DEMOCRACY
and
HALAKHAH

ELIEZER SCHWEID

DEMOCRACY
and
HALAKHAH

UNIVERSITY
PRESS OF
AMERICA

THE JERUSALEM CENTER
FOR PUBLIC AFFAIRS

Lanham • New York • London

Copyright © 1994 by
The Jerusalem Center for Public Affairs

University Press of America®, Inc.
4720 Boston Way
Lanham, Maryland 20706

3 Henrietta Street
London WC2E 8LU England

Co-published by arrangement with
The Jerusalem Center for Public Affairs

Managing Editor: Mark Ami-El
Typesetting: Custom Graphics and Publishing, Ltd., Jerusalem

Library of Congress Cataloging-in-Publication Data

Schweid, Eliezer.
Democracy and halakhah / by Eliezer Schweid.
p.   cm. — (The Milken library of Jewish public affairs)
Includes bibliographical references and index.
1. Judaism and state.   2. Jewish nationalism.   3. Democracy—
Religious aspects—Judaism.   4. Religious Zionism.
5. Hirshenzon, Hayim, 1857–1935.   I. Title.   II. Series.
BM538.S7S37   1994   296.3'877—dc20   93–38732 CIP

ISBN 0–8191–9360–7 (cloth : alk. paper)
ISBN 0–8191–9430–1 (pbk. : alk. paper)

 The paper used in this publication meets the minimum requirements of
American National Standard for Information Sciences—Permanence
of Paper for Printed Library Materials, ANSI Z39.48–1984.

A memorial for my late father-in-law,
Yaakov Fuchs,
who was murdered by the Nazis
on the 9th of Tammuz, 5705,
one of the six million.

THE MILKEN LIBRARY OF JEWISH PUBLIC AFFAIRS

Made possible by a gift from the
Foundations of the Milken Families

CONTENTS

FOREWORD

Daniel J. Elazar

As part of its impact, the modern epoch led to an unprecedented struggle between religion and nationalism within the Jewish people. Probably for the first time in history, nationalism became an independent, secular force in Jewish life. The struggle passed through periods of secularization and assimilation. It reached its apotheosis in the Zionist enterprise, which tried to offer a comprehensive Jewish solution to the modern situation independent of Jewish religious belief.

Until the seventeenth century, Jews perceived themselves and were perceived by others to be a nation defined by their own constitutional law and tradition, formally anchored in its religous system. The secularization of Western society (civil society, as it came to be known after the seventeenth century) resulted in pressing religion into the private sphere, thereby allowing the inauguration of a new, fully secular, basis for national identity in the world. Increasingly, in Western Europe and North America the Jewish response to this was to take on a more limited religious identity for themselves while transferring their national identity to the states in which they became citizens, more or less.

Though this took place in fits and starts, the general thrust was clear. Jews in Eastern Europe who became conscious of the problem sought secular ethnic ways to preserve Jewish nationalism, often rejecting its religious dimension for one modern ideology or another. In time theirs became the principal direction of the Zionist enterprise.

Throughout, however, there were those in both West and East who sought to retain the organic link between religion and nationalism characteristic of the Jewish path. Some sought to do so by preserving the old ways, as they understood them, unchanged. In due course they became the ultra-Orthodox of today, itself a new response to modernity. Still others sought to reconcile the two forces in new ways in the society in the new context of modernity.

Many of them became part of the Mizrachi religious Zionist movement, presenting their views of the situation and its possibilities as part of the Zionist polemic arguments of the late nineteenth and early twentieth centuries.

Few, if any, tried to build a sturdy political-theological bridge on a philosophic basis that could possibly reconcile the Torah — the Jewish constitution — with the transformation forced upon the Jewish people by modernity so as to come out with a coherent, systematic system of political thought that could encompass both. One of the few was Rabbi Haim Hirschensohn, one of those great but almost forgotten men of early Zionist history who, Eliezer Schweid argues and I concur, undertook one of the most comprehensive efforts of anyone to demonstrate how the traditional Torah and modern democracy went hand-in-hand, and as such could, and indeed must, serve as the foundation for the restored Jewish national home. In this rich little volume, Professor Schweid indicates how Rabbi Hirschensohn was not afraid to tackle the most difficult questions posed by modernity, nor did he fail to provide bold and daring responses to them from inside the system of Jewish law.

Born in Safed, Eretz Israel, in 1857, Hirschensohn was among the band of Hebrew cultural pioneers who laid the foundation for the Zionist enterprise. He left the country for good fifty years later feeling himself driven out by the fanatic Ashkenazi religious community in Jerusalem, and after some wanderings ended up as an Orthodox rabbi in Hoboken, New Jersey. There he spent the last quarter of his life and wrote his most comprehensive works, *Malkhi Bakodesh* and *Eileh Divrei Habrit*, two multi-volume works offering a comprehensive religio-national view of a restored Jewish polity in a new world order.

Because of Hirschensohn's particular fate and despite his long struggle to break into the mainstream of Zionist thought and action, his works were all but lost to the Jewish world. The principal Zionist advocates of his time either never found his work or did not bother to seriously explore it. They were fighting other battles and his traditionalism and comprehensiveness took him out of the mainstream. Indeed, none rose to his level of thought, struggling with each other on a much lower level of politics and polemics.

Only years later did Eliezer Schweid come upon these and Hirschensohn's other works discussed in this book and immediately was drawn to them. As it happens, he and I discovered Hirschensohn at roughly the same time. Both of us were entranced by the man and his ideas. But Professor Schweid sat down to do the analysis that we both hoped would begin to restore Hirschensohn's place in Jewish political thought. This book, originally published in Hebrew as *Democratia v'Halakhah*, now continues that effort by bringing Hirschensohn's works to the English-reading public for the first time.

In the following pages, Professor Schweid presents Hirschensohn's ideas showing how they are rooted in the idea of the Torah as the constitutional covenant of the Jewish people. He shows how Hirschensohn built his system on the ideas of covenant and constitution, democracy, and self-organization. Those ideas give us not only food for thought, but a basis for the continuity of a Jewish nationalism formed by the Jews' covenants, rooted in traditional Judaism yet expanded and transformed to deal with the problems of our times.

Haim Hirschensohn stands squarely in the Jewish political tradition. Indeed, his works show him to be one of the missing links in the chain of tradition, both in life and in thought: a Zionist, who unlike other Zionists did not try to transform Jews into secular ethnic nationalists; who sees in the tradition that the Jews have inherited a basis for continuity and the achievement of the restoration of independent Jewish statehood. His work finds its echo in the works of the Fellows at the Jerusalem Center for Public Affairs, among them Professor Schweid, and their colleagues who are today exploring the Jewish political tradition, focusing on precisely those aspects of continuity and change. In these and other respects, he is one of the intellectual fathers of us all.

Haim Hirschensohn exemplifies yet another aspect of the Zionist experience. He was born and lived to middle-age in the Eretz Israel of the first Zionist founding before Zionism fell into the hands of those who sought to radically uproot traditional Jewish religious nationalism and to substitute for it a more-or-less undiluted secular nationalism. Contemporary Israel's first founding covered nearly two generations, from the restoration of Ottoman rule in Eretz Israel (1839-40) to before World War I. In those first generations, three groups took upon themselves the founding of major autonomous Jewish settlements in the land. The first group were Sephardim from the Ottoman empire itself, the Mediterranean world, and Western Asia who brought with them the modern yet comprehensive religious traditionalism of their world and a way of life based on community and commerce which sustained them for centuries. The second consisted of ultra-Orthodox Ashkenazim such as the students of the Vilna Gaon from Lithuania, various Hassidic groups from Galicia, and Hungarian ultra-Orthodox, both of the latter from the Austro-Hungarian empire, who came as part of a negative response to emancipation to build their own self-contained communities best characterized as fundamentalist religious utopias. The third group consisted of the first consciously-proclaimed Zionists from Hibbat Zion and Hovevei Zion, primarily from Russia, who came to settle the land in the spirit of the Russian "back to the land" movement and thus restore a "normal" Jewish presence in the country. Despite the major differences between these three groups, they all had in common a desire to reconcile Jewish tradition with resettlement of the land, each in its own way.

The first generation, between 1840 and 1880, was dominated by the first two of these groups who succeeded in building an infrastructure upon which subsequent Zionist generations could build. The last group dominated the second generation from 1880 to World War I, a period of establishing the first agricultural colonies on the land and the first wave of conscious Zionist resettlement efforts. The first generation brought the establishment of hospitals, newspapers, Western-style schools, roads, railroads, and telecommunications with the outside world. The second led to three concentrations of Jewish agricultural settlement that became known in the West as "the Jewish colonies in Palestine" — on the Mediterranean coast between Jaffa and Haifa, southeast of Jaffa, and in the Upper Gallilee. (Other less successful efforts were attempted around Jerusalem and on the Golan Heights.)

Examining the history, constitutional documents, and even the architecture of these enterprises, one discovers that, unlike later generations of Zionists whose leaders jettisoned Judaism, these three groups developed their communities within the framework and the continuity of the Jewish political tradition. They modeled their communal and settlement covenants on the *takkanot* and *askamot* of their late medieval and early modern predecessors with a greater or lesser degree of modernization, depending on the group. They built synagogues, prayer halls and traditional study halls at the center of their new settlements, rural as well as urban. They established at least basic communal standards for the observance of the Sabbath, festivals, and Jewish public observances in the religious spirit of the new Jewish nationalist enterprise.

One need only read the founding covenants or constitutional documents of the early settlements like Petah Tikva, Rishon le-Zion, and Rehovot, or such urban neighborhoods as Neve Zedek, Nahalat Shiva and Mea Shearim to see this, black on white. As increasingly historical-minded later generations go back to restore the old buildings of these first generations of settlement, the old synagogues are being rediscovered for the architectural gems that they are. Prior to the coming of the second aliyah, the first of the revolutionary socialist *aliyot* from Russia and Russian Poland that ultimately put a stop to this effort at continuity and synthesis, it was the continuity and synthesis which prevailed.

Haim Hirschensohn wrote as the son of the first of those generations and accurately reflected and expanded upon the thinking of the second. He felt himself forced to leave Eretz Israel precisely at the time when the first of these groups were pushed aside by the new Zionists, the second completely turned toward what became ultra-Orthodoxy, and the third was swallowed up by the young revolutionaries. Thus his ideas were pushed far from what became the Zionist mainstream. But his thought also suggests to us the promise of what could have been, and brings us back to a better understanding of how the first founding of modern Israel began.

Professor Schweid has done us all a great service by putting the thoughts of Rabbi Haim Hirschensohn in our hands in such a convenient way. This book deserves to be read widely and to become a catalyst for the republication of Hirschensohn's works in Hebrew and in translation into English. The Jerusalem Center for Public Affairs is extraordinarily proud to be an instrument in this effort.

PREFACE

This monograph is the outcome of a comprehensive program of research on Jewish national thought in Eretz Israel during the first half of the twentieth century. Among the many "discoveries" which I found in that wonderful "archive" known as Hebrew literature during the period of the revival were the essays of a prolific writer, the late Rabbi Haim Hirschensohn. Readily available, these thoughtful and impressive essays drew little attention at the time and upon their publication were immediately forgotten and given no further thought. What explanation can there be? Is this an indication of some enduring failure in our spiritual life?

My research uncovered quite a number of important, long-forgotten works, but it was the extensive works of Rabbi Hirschensohn that aroused special excitement. For some time I had wondered how it was that religious Zionism had not produced a philosopher and theoretician who dared to confront the complex problems of establishing a modern Jewish state according to *halakhic* concepts. How could it be that we still had no evidence of a comprehensive and systematic attempt to lay a *halakhic* foundation for a democratic, theological and political regime?

Here, full of daring and energy — in Rabbi Hirschensohn's work — such an attempt does exist. Presented in a simple and clear manner, it is first and foremost a formulation of basic questions: Is it possible to establish, on the basis of *halakhah*, a democratic Jewish state which rests its legislative authority on the will of the people, and which develops a modern economy, modern social organizations, culture and art to their full extent? Can the Torah guide the actions of a sovereign, political people? Is there a way to reach a general national consensus on the basis of this doctrine? These are questions which we repeatedly encounter, both in theory and in practice. Certainly, much has been written on these issues, but most of it has been journalistic, enmeshed in the storms of partisan controversy without dealing with the basics. There is still very little written material which attempts to come to grips with fundamental problems in order to propose solutions which are based both on an assessment of reality and on an interpretation of *halakhah*. From this aspect, the work of Rabbi Hirschensohn, in its broad scope and depth, is a rare find.

More than forty years after the establishment of the State of Israel, Rabbi Hirschensohn's solutions are not, of course, adequate. The reality which has emerged is much more complex than could have been foreseen in the 1920s and 1930s. But the way in which he presented the issues, and the principles with which he approached their solution, can still be productive. They can promote public understanding and perhaps bring real solutions closer. Thus, I consider the writing of this book on Rabbi Hirschensohn's theories a fulfillment of the commandment of reuniting a lost article with its owners.

Several good friends helped me fulfill this commandment. First among them is Dr. Ezra Ben Gershom, whose interest in the subjects I was working on stimulated my thoughts and whose financial contribution permitted the publication of the book. I also received much assistance from Rabbi Hirschensohn's daughter, the late Mrs. Tamar de Sola Pool. Since I met her concerning my research into her father's writings, she accompanied the preparation of this monograph and greatly assisted in its publication in Hebrew.

It was the late Mrs. de Sola Pool's and my own ardent wish that this book be available for the interested public of English readers. It seemed that its translation and publication should be considered an act of justice both to the blessed memory of a rabbi who was dedicated to his American Jewish community, and to the community which nurtured within it this most important contribution to modern Jewish philosophical and *halakhic* thought. However, it took much time to overcome the difficulties and to find a suitable way of implementation. It is, indeed, to the merit of Prof. Daniel Elazar, President of the Jerusalem Center for Public Affairs, and of Mr. Zvi Marom, its Director-General, that this double moral debt is finally settled. Special thanks are due also to Mr. Amnon Hadary for his excellent translation.

I extend my feelings of gratitude and appreciation for all those, mentioned or unmentioned, who contributed to the writing, the translating and the publishing of this book. My wish is that the positive responses of many readers will be their due reward.

Eliezer Schweid
February 1992

INTRODUCTION

Rabbi Haim Hirschensohn was a theoretician, a researcher and an original philosopher. He was very active in the religious Zionist movement, especially in the field of education, and left behind him a prodigious literary outpouring. Born in Safed, educated in Jerusalem, he served as the rabbi of a congregation in the United States. His writings and activity were marked by originality and daring, clarity, precision and depth in a fascinating confrontation with the basic issues surrounding the renaissance of the Jewish people in the modern era: issues of political rebirth, social revival, and cultural and religious resurgence. Among broad circles of scholars, leaders and intellectuals, his ideas aroused keen interest and reactions, both of agreement and criticism.

Hirschensohn was an audacious pioneer who confronted the question of the Jewish nature of a modern Jewish state from a theological-*halakhic* viewpoint. His essays demonstrate a thorough deliberation, a quest for positive solutions to the myriad issues which the State of Israel has been attempting to resolve over the years. As early as the period of the Balfour Declaration, he was prescient in his conjectures as to the grave *halakhic* questions which would arise, and he promptly began preparing the tools for their solution. Nonetheless, the man and his life work remain completely unknown to most people. His essays did not win more than superficial journalistic review and, even though discussions and arguments arose from time to time, his profound reflections stayed within his private correspondence and did not find their way into the public debate. This is an astonishing, if not unusual, fact which historians will have to weigh. This essay is not meant as a history. Its intention is to try to reunite a cherished loss with its owners while there may still be time to put it to good use on their behalf.

Who, then, was this man? What is the background to his work? What was the range of his work? The following is not intended to be a complete biography, although this would also be an important task for a historian of Jewish settlement in Eretz Israel. Presented here is only the minimal factual background necessary for an understanding of the philosophical theory to which the main parts of this monograph are devoted.

Rabbi Haim Hirschensohn was born in Safed in 1857.[1] His parents, who were among the first of the Hibbat Zion settlers, immigrated to Eretz Israel from Pinsk in 1847, and the boy grew up in an atmosphere of love of Torah, of Eretz Israel and of the Hebrew language. The broad-mindedness and tolerance which characterize his philosophy had their roots in the atmosphere of his parents' home. In 1864,[2] following the earthquake in Safed, the family settled in Jerusalem. The father was an outstanding Torah scholar, author of several books,[3] and a founder and principal of the Succat Shalom Yeshiva. Haim, who began studying Torah with the scholar Rabbi Berl Merkis,[4] became his father's pupil by the age of twelve.[5] Indeed, throughout his lifetime, both in his religious and national views, and in his study of Torah,[6] he continued to consider himself a student and follower of his father. He was eighteen when he married Chava Sarah, the daughter of Rabbi Shaul Binyamin HaCohen, a founder and principal of the Etz Haim Yeshiva in Jerusalem. Their family life, as described in Rabbi Hirschensohn's essays,[7] was exemplary. Chava Sarah participated in her husband's work and spiritual output as he devoted his energies to writing and public activity.

In the early years, Hirschensohn did not consider using his knowledge of Torah to earn a livelihood. He tried his hand at a number of small factories (printing, soap, beds) with little success. In 1885 he set out on a trip abroad, visiting relatives in Russia and Germany. While in Frankfurt-am-Main, he was impressed by the literature of the Science of Judaism, made contact with some of its proponents and began to publish the monthly, *HaMisdarona* (Through the Corridor). The journal continued to appear in Jerusalem for the next four years, after which it ceased publication due to lack of funds.

On his return to Eretz Israel, Hirschensohn's activities turned to literary and public works, and in both areas he gravitated toward education. His goal was to bridge the gap that had been created between Torah and life, between religion and nationalism, between a tradition of the past and a present which was already anticipating a new future. The monthly, *HaMisdarona*, was dedicated to research into Judaism; its uniqueness lay not only in being the first of its kind in Jerusalem, but in its contemporary national outlook. In the journal, Hirschensohn wanted to deal with the problem of reviving a Torah scholarship which could lay the foundations for national life, rather than a scholarship which was an ideal for individuals who were isolated from the people. In his opinion, the crisis in traditional scholarship arose from the expanding horizons of the Enlightenment, as well as from modern economic conditions. The majority of Jews could no longer devote their free time to Torah study, so ways had to be found to give people a basic Torah education sufficient enough to lead a Torah way of life under new conditions. The name *HaMisdarona* reflects the desire to find an appropriate course of study or discipline.[8] It was to this issue that Hirschensohn devoted his early works, such as *Syllabus of Talmudic Studies for Beginners*,[9] and *An Explanation of Attributes*.[10] This was an attempt to harness the research work of the Science of Judaism to the plow of educational effort as it struggled with the problems of modern life.

Nor did Hirschensohn stop at literary activity alone. Together with Eliezer Ben Yehuda, Rabbi Yaakov Meir, Rabbi Yehiel Michal Pines and Rabbi David Yellin, he founded "Safah Brurah," the "Clear Language" Association, to promote spoken Hebrew. As in Ben Yehuda's home, the members of Hirschensohn's family took it upon themselves to speak Hebrew at home, and Hirschensohn was particularly proud of his wife's role in educating their children entirely in Hebrew.[11] Indeed, he was faithful to Hebrew all his life, writing in Hebrew and educating his children and grandchildren to speak Hebrew even when he lived in Exile, in the United States. Spoken Hebrew, he felt, was the necessary basis for a national-religious education in Judaism; thus he devoted much of his literary effort to Hebrew instruction and to Hebrew education. As a teacher at the "Lemel" school in Jerusalem, he became interested in putting this educational theory into practice. He was opposed by extremists whose great dissatisfaction was aroused by his concerted efforts with Ben Yehuda to revive Hebrew speech, and by his association, as supervisor and board member, with the Herzberg Orphanage Home whose founders, though Orthodox Jews from Germany, were held suspect by the extremists. There was much agitation, and matters even reached a declaration of excommunication.[12]

Did this controversy, or the generally constrictive spiritual atmosphere which he felt among the Orthodox community in Jerusalem, cause him to leave Eretz Israel? In any case, following this incident, in 1901, Hirschensohn left for Constantinople where he took over the directorship of two Hebrew schools, Tiferet Zvi and Or Torah. This was an important opportunity for him to deal with modern Jewish educational problems. For example, these were schools in which all subjects were taught in Hebrew. Preliminary work was required to determine curricula, develop educational systems and even write textbooks. Hirschensohn took all this upon himself, and his original work remains a noteworthy chapter in the history of Hebrew education.[13]

There is an interesting note about this transitional period which influenced the development of his philosophical world view. Hirschensohn was motivated by the lectures of a local adherent of the Jewish Enlightenment and began a critical study of Spinoza and his theory. Since the Hebrew translation then extant, of Dr. Rubin, seemed to him to be imprecise, he used the German translation, transposing it into Hebrew by himself and adding his own notes. He continued with the project until he had satisfied his interest, at which point he stopped.[14] At the same time he was also engaged in a systematic study of the Rambam's *Guide of the Perplexed*.[15] In the confrontation between Spinoza's critique and the study of Rambam, his own views as a theologian were crystallized.

Hirschensohn was among the first to join the Mizrahi movement and saw himself as a founder of the organization. He had been in close contact with Rabbi Reines and subsequently with Mizrahi leaders in the United States.[16] However, during his years in the United States, it is true that he was kept out of political activity in the movement. There is a hint of a controversy in his letters concerning Mizrahi's place in the World Zionist Organization, and one gets the impression that there was a deliberate attempt to keep him at a distance from the central institutions of the movement. This is an issue which deserves careful scrutiny at another time.[17] In any case, throughout his life, Hirschensohn remained an active member of Mizrahi. During his stay in Constantinople he was chosen as a delegate to the Sixth Zionist Congress in Basel. There he met delegates from the United States and was persuaded to move to America, together with his family.

That was at the end of 1903. After a short period, he was installed as the rabbi of an Orthodox community in Hoboken, New Jersey, a position in which he continued until his death in 1935. By and large, Hirschensohn's life in the United States was a long period of quiet creativity. Even there, however, he came across religious extremism. His book, *Yamim M'Kedem* (Days of Yore), which was published in 1907 aroused a zealous scholar in New York to publicize a derogatory letter;[18] however, the Orthodox Rabbinical Assembly supported Hirschensohn. If one can judge by the number of testimonies in Hirschensohn's own books,[19] he met with success as a rabbi and earned the respect of his congregation; thus, he was able to devote himself to his wide-ranging literary work. Several of the essays which he mentions in his published works were not printed (among them, by the way, a large volume of poems, several of which he had included in published essays); many were published, probably with the assistance of his congregation.[20]

The following is a list of the principal published works which were researched for the present volume. Hirschensohn's literary activity began at a very young age. When he was seventeen, he wrote *Ateret Zkeinim* (Glory of the Aged). Although the impression one has from his remarks is that the book was published, it is not found in the National Library in Jerusalem. The first publication we have is the journal, *HaMisdarona* (Through the Corridor), followed by *Seder Hoshanot Im Beiur Yeshuot Yaakov* (The Prayer Book for Hoshanot with Explanations), 1887; *Seder HaTalmud L'Mathilim* (Syllabus of Talmud Studies for Beginners), 1891; *Yamim M'Kedem* (Days of Yore), 1908; *Hidushei Rav Hirschensohn Al Masekhet Horayot* (Comments of Rabbi Hirschensohn on Tractate Horayot), 1914-16; *Malki BaKodesh* (My King in the Sanctuary), 1919-28; *Sefer Motzei Mayim* (The Water Drawers), 1924; *Sefer Eileh Divrei HaBrit* (This is the Covenant), 1926-28; *Sefer Torat HaHinukh HaYisraeli* (Theory of Jewish Education), 1927; *Sefer Nimukei Rashi* (The Reasoning of Rashi), 1929; *Sefer Beirurei HaMidot* (An Explanation of the Criteria), 1929-31; *Sefer Musagei Shav V'HaEmet* (Concepts of Truth and Falsehood), 1932; *Seder La'Mikrah* (Syllabus for Bible Study), 1933; *Torat Eretz Yisrael* (The Laws of Eretz Israel), 1935; *Luah Moadei Yisrael Im Haggadah Shel Pesah U'Ve'ur Madai* (A Calendar of Jewish Holidays with the Haggadah of Pesach and Scientific Explanations), 1935.

These writings, some of them large, multi-volumed works, can be divided by their subject matter into the following categories:

1. Oral Law, system and methods of study (especially *Seder HaTalmud L'Mathilim* and *Sefer Beirurei HaMidot*).

2. Biblical research and problems of biblical criticism (especially *Yamim M'Kedem*, *Sefer Nimukei Rashi* and *Sefer La'Mikrah*).

3. Jewish education (especially *Sefer Torat HaHinukh HaYisraeli* and *Luah Moadei Yisrael*).

4. Jewish theology (especially *Sefer Musagei Shav V'HaEmet*).

5. Direct confrontation with questions of the political-national renaissance and the cultural and spiritual revival of the Jewish people in Eretz Israel, the overriding thread of all these works.

In each of the essays listed above there is clearly an attempt to deal with the various problems of the Jewish condition in the modern era. The central volume in this confrontation is the six-part book, *Malki BaKodesh*, followed by *Hidushei Rav Hirschensohn Al Masekhet Horayot* and the three-part work, *Sefer Eileh Divrei HaBrit*.

The book *Malki BaKodesh* is a *halakhic* response to the new historical period which, in Hirschensohn's opinion, began with the advent of the Balfour Declaration. Having observed the rapid changes which occurred in Jewish life since the beginning of Emancipation and Enlightenment, Hirschensohn understood that the future would hold even more rapid and revolutionary changes. It was unavoidable. These changes, however, need not necessarily mean the destruction of Torah Judaism. Depending entirely on what kind of reaction and adaptation occurred, change could bring with it either a blessing or a curse: a blessing if national response was well directed; a curse if the response reflected individual objectives rather than collective national responsibility.

From this point of view, the Balfour Declaration was of great significance because in its aftermath the people were again confronted with a collective national agenda. In other words, responses to specific individuals or isolated communities were no longer sufficient. The questions to be dealt with now concerned the national leadership of a people about to gain its independence. The Balfour Declaration was the foundation of the Jewish state which would soon be established. The excitement of approaching redemption accompanied the writing of *Malki BaKodesh*; it could be said that the Days of the Messiah were at hand. And this was expressed directly, even in the way dates were cited at the beginning of each volume: "In the Second Year of the Recognition by the Allied Governments of our Rights to Eretz Israel." In this, Hirschensohn, without a doubt, was close to the great figure of his generation, Rabbi Avraham Yitzhak HaCohen Kook. However, he saw the vision of redemption in a totally different manner. Whereas Rabbi Kook perceived the sparkling of a meta-historic reality, Hirschensohn regarded it as a historical process. The Jewish state would rise amidst the economic, social and political conditions of modern times. It could, therefore, cause a break in the bond between tradition and contemporary national life just as it could create the conditions for a great spiritual revival. There was room for tremendous hope, as well as a sense of danger, which meant that one could not rely on vision alone. It was necessary to look objectively at what the nature of a modern Jewish state would be. Of course Hirschensohn did not doubt that a Jewish state meant a state which would ensure the national independence of the Jewish people and which would conduct itself according to the Torah. Neither did he doubt that this state, rising as it would within an existing historical reality, would be democratic and that it would be based on scientific achievement, technology and Western social culture. The piercing question, then, was whether these two determinant factors — tradition and modernity — could coexist; in principle, Hirschensohn's answer was positive.

In principle, there was no reason for a schism to develop between Torah and daily life. But the accord between Torah and daily life was not a predetermined course. It must constantly be created, particularly in times of such fundamental changes in social conditions. Yet, at this crucial time, it appeared that the process of *halakhic* thinking had become paralyzed. *Halakhic* scholars were dawdling; they did not accept the task of anticipating changes and preparing the requisite *halakhic* tools. Hirschensohn, therefore, took this pioneering and daring task upon himself. As he sought to prepare the ideological and *halakhic* tools needed to create a constitutional foundation for a modern, democratic Jewish state comported according to the Torah, it became clear that the preparation of these tools involved dealing with a broad range of problems: economic, social and political, on the one hand; scientific, cultural and philosophical, on the other. Hirschensohn's body of work offers detailed answers in all these areas, thus making it of particular moment.

Any biographical introduction must emphasize Hirschensohn's position which was exceptional on two counts: vis-a-vis the reality that had emerged in Eretz Israel and with respect to Jewish public life in the United States. Hirschensohn wrote in Hebrew, and the issues which concerned him were mainly the issues of the Jewish revival in Eretz Israel. In other words, even in Exile, Hirschensohn lived the life of Eretz Israel and wrote for a Hebrew readership that was, in fact, located only in Eretz Israel. His Torah was the Torah of Eretz Israel. Why did he go into Exile? Why didn't he return? He left Eretz Israel, as noted earlier, probably due to a sense of pressure and suffocation from within the Orthodox community. But why didn't he make an effort to return? The question was raised by several people who wrote in response to his book, *Malki BaKodesh;*[21] Hirschensohn's replies were not convincing. Eretz Israel, he said, needs young people who can contribute to its upbuilding. As a middle-aged philosopher, he could contribute to the building of Eretz Israel only if he were materially independent; accordingly, he would return only if he could assure himself an independent economic existence. Apparently he was afraid that he would be unable to continue his literary and public work among Orthodox Jewry in Eretz Israel, and he preferred life in America.

How did he assess American Jewry? In many of his writings there are harsh references to its sad state: the materialism, the neglect of Torah study, the rejection of religious observance, the superficiality of education, etc. Though he attempted to offer avenues for improving the situation, one gets the impression that he did not believe a basic reform of conditions in Exile was possible. From this point of view, he was a consistent Zionist. His trust, his burning faith and the power of his thought were dedicated to endeavors in Eretz Israel.

It would, nonetheless, be a mistake to ignore the positive and consciously decisive influence America had in shaping his world view. A sensitive examination of his writing discloses Hirschensohn's great admiration and love for the democratic culture of America. He saw the culture reflected in the character of its political constitution and the functioning of its judicial, legislative and executive institutions; in the religious tolerance of American society, its ethnic and cultural pluralism; in scientific and technological progress and in the open attitude toward Jews. Hirschensohn saw the danger of assimilation clearly, but at the same time he admired the freedom which was rooted in American democracy. It would not be an exaggeration to say that he considered American democracy the paradigm for the formation of a Torah-led Jewish state. In other words, he discerned that American democracy had been established on biblical principles, principles of a covenantal society. Thus, a Jewish ideologue and philosopher could learn much from its biblical notion of the covenant in order to create a foundation for a modern Torah-led Jewish state.

From the outset, Hirschensohn was characterized by openmindedness and tolerance; he was educated to these traits in his parents' home. However, in America he found a social atmosphere which allowed him to maintain these views, develop and disseminate them, and find the same measure of openness and understanding within his religious Jewish environment. It is doubtful that he could have found a similar atmosphere of respect and understanding had he lived among the ultra-religious community in Eretz Israel. In the United States, Hirschensohn found the enabling framework to develop views which he had acquired through the influence of his parents' national-religious upbringing. The dilemma raised by the fact that he emigrated to the United States in order to write openly about Eretz Israel cannot be ignored. The price was high. He was, in fact, cut off from directly influencing the realization of Zionism in Eretz Israel. At the same time, since he wrote in Hebrew and focused on the problems of Eretz Israel, he also cut himself off from any direct or overall influence on American Jewry. Perhaps that is the basic reason that his dynamic and vibrant works, which discuss pressing problems of the times with great scholarship and depth, did not gain the attention they deserved either in the United States or in Israel.

The purpose of this monograph, then, is to systematically describe and analyze Hirschensohn's world view as it is reflected in the published essays to which we have access. Two qualifications must be emphasized: first, the present survey and analysis is limited to essays printed and available in Jerusalem. It should be stated again that despite the fact that this is a sizeable collection, this material is only a part of a much greater output. In his published works, Hirschensohn mentions other important essays which were only in manuscript form. These expressed his basic ideas as well, and there is no doubt that had we been able to obtain them we could have filled in several lacunae and expanded the scope of subjects discussed. Second, this survey and analysis is limited to a discussion of Hirschensohn's systematic world view and does not go into detail about distinct professional areas. I refer here to the history of the Jewish people; biblical exegesis and criticism; and chiefly, research into the Oral Law, its tools and methods, and *halakhic* discourse. Hirschensohn made significant contributions in all of these fields. His books are filled with ideas relating to the objective explication of issues of ancient Jewish history, biblical exegesis and formulation of the biblical text, and methods of Oral Law and its principles. His responses to questions which arose in daily life were based on detailed *halakhic* judgements. We could not go into detail in these subjects, partly because of considerations of space and partly because of a lack of specific professional skills, mainly in the areas of research into Oral Law and *halakhic* interpretation. A specialist in this field must deal with this aspect.

It is, of course, impossible not to touch on these topics, but the focus of this monograph is on the general theoretical approaches and ideological principles which guided Hirschensohn's research and *halakhic* deliberations, rather than the research or *halakhic* deliberations themselves.

Notes

1. G. Krassel, *Lexicon of Hebrew Literature* (Merhavia, 1965), Vol. 1, entry on Haim Hirschensohn.
2. Yosef Gavrieli, "Genius and Student of Talmud (The Late Rabbi Haim Hirschensohn, Thirty Years after his Death)," *HaTzofeh*, 1965.
3. *Succat Shalom, Dvar HaShmittah, Mei Be'er, Kedushat Eretz Israel*, and others.
4. Rabbi Hirschensohn, *Eileh Divrei HaBrit*, Sec. 3, p. 6.
5. Rabbi Hirschensohn, *Hidushei Hirschensohn Horayot*, p. 50.
6. See his letter to Rabbi Abba Citron, *Malki BaKodesh*, Sec. 4.
7. See the testimony of Rabbi Hirschensohn, as well as of his children, in the book *Musagei Shav V'HaEmet*.
8. See the opening article of the first issue of *HaMisdarona*.
9. Jerusalem, 1891.
10. Jerusalem, 1928-31.
11. See "El Banei U'Venotei," *Malki BaKodesh*, end of Sec. A.
12. G. Krassel, *op. cit.*
13. See his remarks in *Torat HaHinuch HaYisraeli*, Ch. 2, Sec. 4.
14. See *Musagei Shav V'HaEmet*, end of Sec. C.
15. *Ibid.*, Introductions to Sec. C and E.
16. See his remarks in "El Banei U'Venotei," in *Malki BaKodesh*, end of Part 1. Also, the letter to Yosef Ben Zion, in "Babad," *Malki BaKodesh*, Part 6.
17. Such suggestions appear in several letters in *Malki BaKodesh*, Sec. D.
18. See Hirschenson's remarks in the booklet, "Aneh K'sil" ("Answer a Fool") [no date or place of publication].
19. See the introduction by Hirschensohn, and those in English by Sol Louvash and Rabbi Leon Shpitz, in *Beirurei HaMidot*, Part 1.
20. On his seventieth birthday, members of Rabbi Hirschensohn's congregation established a fund for the publication of his books. See *ibid.*
21. For instance, the letter to Abba Citron, *Malki BaKodesh*, Part 4.

Chapter 1

THE CHALLENGE OF MODERN ISSUES

Haim Hirschensohn's writing is characteristically that of a *halakh-ist* both in its style and in its form of response to topics which were of concern to him. He addressed political, social, cultural and theological subjects which came directly out of daily life in a prescient response to the burning questions of the modern period. His uniqueness as a theoretician is evident in his attempts to anticipate major issues and his desire to prove that there was no modern dilemma for which a positive, Torah-based solution could not be found.

Hirschensohn's alertness to the rapid historical changes which were occurring in the life of the Jewish people has already been noted. In the space of a very brief period at the beginning of the modern era, changes took place which were greater than those that had occurred in the past over much longer periods of time, and it could be assumed that the future would see an increase in the rate of acceleration.[1] What were the causes of change and in what direction were they headed? Hirschensohn did not usually answer in generalizations, preferring to relate to specific issues. In only one place can an attempt to offer a general historical overview be found, and this should be presented in its entirety as a background to a discussion of specific issues.

Anyone who is concerned with the condition of the Jewish people, who is open and seeks to account for each situation with a penetrating eye, and who is logical, knows that the reason for the spiritual chaos prevalent in the last generation was a lack of "communal strength" among our people. Over the last 150 years, many have attributed this weakness to the result of the Ben Menachem version of Haskalah [Enlightenment],[2] and the general historical process of civilization in the world. Man has ceased to rely on the expertise of others; ours is a generation in which each individual considers himself wise despite the fact that he does not understand deeply and is not faithful to God. Some attribute the decline to Emancipation in general, saying

1

that the strength of the Jewish community existed when it "was a people which dwelt alone," and had nothing to do with other nations. In those days there was a special strength in their own centers of life — in their synagogues, their schools, their separate streets and the villages in which the majority was Jewish. However, when Jews were allowed to mix with the gentile community, the glory of the *kahal,* which had been kept as a separate and distinct center unto itself, declined. From that time on, Jews were considered as part of the people in whose midst they lived, whether for good, as the assimilationists thought, or for bad; in any case, religious Jews looked upon this with pain and a knowing nod. Yet others placed the blame for the breakdown of the community on the community itself: on community leaders who were overly authoritarian and shortsighted, who did not understand either what the future held or the changes that were taking place in the world at large. They held people in such tight check that the bonds were torn.

Indeed, all three opinions are correct. The current community leadership is not acting wisely by leading the people with moderation or preparing them for the changing times. Emancipation need not have disrupted the community at all; on the contrary, the human rights which were given directly to every people without distinction as to race, religion or status,[3] were rights not only of the individual but collectively of every race, religion and class. What was required was a reconceptualization of the community which would correspond to the changes occurring in the country. To our sorrow, we did not have spiritual leaders great enough to chart this new course.

Therefore, the light of Enlightenment brought with it thousands of shadows, or misleading lights, and regretfully the Jewish people were cast into total anarchy. Each person did whatever he thought best, acting not for himself alone but attempting to influence others to do what he thought correct, even though the end result could not be known. Communities split into many factions — Reform, Orthodox, a Hassidic group, groups "in between," and "combatants."[4] The truth was absent. Might became right, not through the strength of the community but through personal power, a power of the arrogance of youth before elders, and the contemptible lording it over the noble. This caused the chaos and darkness which has overcome the

Jewish people in Exile, and also of late, to our sorrow, in Eretz Israel.

I believed and still believe, true to my faith, that the spirit of God hovers on the face of the living waters of our Holy Torah. If only the leaders of the community had not abandoned the ways of Torah in matters of public law; if, as noted in Tractate Shabbat 139-1, the ignorant had not taken the law into their own hands, not with accord to a genuine study of Torah, not as true service but as lip service in order to trample underfoot a holy people; if only the present leadership had paid as much attention as earlier leaders to this part of *halakhah* — according to the principles of the Jerusalem and Babylonian Talmuds — then the Enlightenment would also have been a godsend, and equality of rights would have strengthened us. Then all the nations would have recognized us as a kingdom of priests and a holy people, and would have said that this is a wise and clever people. Only one component was missing, the component of communal power, and that caused the spiritual destruction within us in all the lands of Exile.

The *kahal* was not an innovation of Exile, created when the Jews lost the physical center of their peoplehood, as many mistakenly think. "Community" precedes the concept of people. In Egypt, it was said that the entire community of Israel would perform [the Passover] (Exodus 12:6). The principle of community is a basic principle and a foundation of our nationhood and religion, and the dissolution of the power of the community has caused great upheaval. In the United States, we see that any desecration of the sanctity of religion or demeaning of the honor of the Torah owing to our great sins, comes from the lack of an organized community which the *government*[5] can recognize as expert and authoritative in everything pertaining to the Jewish religion; at the same time, Eretz Israel lacks a community organization which *the people* wholeheartedly recognize as their authority. Indeed, these authorities must be constituted according to *halakhah*, which would endow them with legitimate authority and power that would be binding on the entire community.[6]

In this section, which was written as the introduction to a *halakhic* discussion on the authority of Jewish leadership, emphasis is on the lack of "community power," i.e., the disintegration of the authority of public leadership. This is distinctive of Hirschensohn's decidedly Zionist approach. His belief that a national revival in Eretz Israel was the precondition to any solution was based on the assumption that it would be possible to meet all the challenges of the modern era if the Jewish people would renew its communal framework and authoritative national leadership. Indeed, this assumption stood at the core of an important part of his work. Also in this section, his opinion on two decisive external changes is to be found: the Enlightenment, i.e., the penetration of secular culture into the sphere of Jewish spiritual life; and the Emancipation, i.e., the integration of Jews into a social environment open to them. Added to this, one must consider the impact of an external way of life which is marked by two prominent phenomena: materialism as a social value, and extreme individualism.

For Hirschensohn, all these phenomena characterized the modern era and demanded a new configuration from the Jewish leadership, so that the direction of change could be guided away from the destruction of national and religious life to its renewal. Hirschensohn's attitude towards Emancipation was, as noted, positive. Moreover, he considered the modern national movement in Eretz Israel to be a clear reflection of the process of Emancipation. As noted above, the idea of equal rights held within it the possibility for strengthening the power of the Jewish people's center. In other words, a change occurred in the relationship of the peoples of the world to the Jewish people's aspirations for national redemption, and the way was open for the fulfillment of the hope that the Jewish people would once again be an independent people in its own land. In this sense, the Balfour Declaration was also a reflection of the process of historical progress inherent in Emancipation.

Hirschensohn considered the Jewish struggle for an independent Jewish life a clear expression of Emancipation in its aspiration to encompass, within the framework of Jewish cultural creativity, areas which had been outside the ghetto parameters throughout the entire period of Exile. Emancipation, in this sense, meant new responsibility — total and comprehensive — for a state, a society, an economy and a complete cultural entity. That was the full scope of the change wrought by the national movement, itself a function of Emancipation. Nor did Hirschensohn see a need to justify his position; it was for him self-evident. The justification of the national movement as a movement whose goal was independence and creativity in various walks of life was rooted in the original essence of Judaism as he understood it: "Torath Haim," a law designed for fullness of life. Hirschensohn did not ignore the problems which arose as a result of national Emancipation and the need for a reorganization in order to deal with them. The responsibility for a state, a society and a culture posits these spheres of activity as areas with an inherent value, adding to those features which already distinguish traditional Judaism, revealing vital values beyond the narrow, traditional limits of religion. As a result, the relationship between the religious component and the national component in Jewish life necessarily changed; the national component, including those spheres outside religion, became independent, even to be seen as a desirable goal in itself. It was not astonishing, therefore, that Jews who dedicated themselves to these activities would see them as more important than religion.[7] At any rate, a distinction which pre-Emancipation Jews had not recognized developed between the national aspect and the religious aspect of Judaism. Moreover, a sector evolved within the Jewish people that defined its tie to Judaism solely on the basis of its national affiliation, as distinct from Jews who defined their connection to Judaism solely on the basis of religion. This was the height of danger and it had to be faced from the viewpoint of religious nationalism.

The inroad made by secular culture was part of the phenomenon described above, but it raised special problems. First, the competition between the demands of a general education and the demands of Torah scholarship; and second, the influence of the humanities, especially historical and philological research, on Jewish studies. In several instances, this influence was the cause of confusion, for it undermined the authority of the sacred writings and set in doubt beliefs which in the past had been held within the sanctity of religion.

Finally, there was the enticement of a materialistic lifestyle in an open society. This phenomenon was thrust at Hirschensohn with full force, especially in the United States. He himself saw a rapid process of destruction: the community, the family, observance of the commandments, the Jewish education of children, study of Torah — all these were swept away through the ambition for material achievement, convenience and in an imitation of the surroundings.

5

How could one deal with these difficult issues? This is the question which Hirschensohn sought to answer as a scholar, an ideologue and a *halakhist*.

Notes

1. See *Malki BaKodesh*, Part 1, "El Banei U'Venotei."
2. The reference is to a system of education based on the (Moshe ben Menachem) Mendelssohn school of thought.
3. The reference is to Class: proletariat, property owner, etc.
4. Those "in between" (*geshari*) were a reference to the Conservatives, who bridged the two camps; "combatants" (*maarakhthi*) may have referred to the secular nationalists who waged a battle against religion.
5. Emphasis by the author.
6. *Hidushei Rav Hirschensohn Al Masekhet Horayot*; the Preface is entitled "Healem Dvar Shel Tzibur!"
7. Statements of this nature appear in *HaMisdarona*, Vol. 3, No. 1, in the article, "Hesderim Ba'Halakhah V'Ahavat HaMelakhah," and on the importance of independent national values in *Malki BaKodesh*, Sec. B, Question B, regarding unenforceable political decrees.

Chapter 2

THE MEANING OF NATIONALISM

Haim Hirschensohn's reaction to the condition of the Jewish people in the modern era is apparent in his views on Jewish nationalism. Of particular importance is the change that occurred in his thinking after he experienced Jewish life in the United States. Initially, Hirschensohn accepted the Mizrahi movement's point of view that a complete identity exists between nationalism and religion within Judaism: the religion is essentially national and nationalism is essentially religious. These two systems are connected through the Torah which is the covenantal document establishing the people before God. Even at this early stage, however, Hirschensohn's writings reveal a depth and openness to unusual directions, and his conclusions reflect several original ideas in the area of ethical and religious thought, and in the field of *halakhah*.

In what sense is the Jewish religion a national religion? One should begin with a negative determination. According to Hirschensohn, Jewish religion is distinct from Christianity in that it has neither a dogma nor is it organized on ecclesiastical lines. Faith in Judaism stands the test of reason, and the Jew is commanded to examine the truth; he is not *a priori* commanded to accept any teaching. Consequently, if one strays from the basics of faith, he is not considered immediately a heretic. The issues on which Torah education focuses are the qualities of devotion, awe, love of one's fellow-man and search for the truth. These are concerns which relate to practical behavior and not to ideas. The Jewish religion does, indeed, demand a specific way of life, and the Torah is the compilation of commandments which guides man within his society in all his actions. It is at this point that religion and nationality are connected because the way of life which the Torah mandates relates to the individual's role within the people and to the people as an entity. The idea is not a new one, but its inestimable importance is emphasized in connection with national-religious ideology.

Hirschensohn's enthusiasm for the national revival of the Jewish people stems equally from the aspiration for political independence

7

and sovereignty similar to that of other peoples, and from the internal significance of nationality, in the sense of a society's self-organization. Only a community which has the "power to organize" itself can be called by the term "people." Nationalism is expressed through direction-giving legislative institutions in all areas of life; individuals act out their freedom through a voluntary association with society, thereby exercising their selfhood.[1] Hirschensohn, therefore, emphasized democracy, rather than sovereignty, as the ultimate expression of national life, and it is instructive that the *religious* aspect of nationality emphasizes this point. The Torah of Israel has the force of a covenant of the people before God, [in which]:

> ...an individual annuls his ego for the sake of the whole community, each one is held responsible for the whole...and consequently our obligations to the Torah and the commandments are basically the bond and the Covenant which we made concerning the totality of God's commandments. This was not done by the power of the sages, the judges and the elders of the people because if it had come through their power, it would be as a decree rather than a voluntary acceptance, and this voluntary acceptance was God's main desire. Only after all the people had entered the Covenant and voluntarily taken the oath did they then choose judges and elders who would stand guard over their observance, just as in the adoption of any constitution.
>
> In my humble opinion, this is the underpinning for one of the great principles of Jewish faith — of its religion and nationality; it is a pillar of the entire Torah and the commandments. It is one of the basics of our faith that God has no quarrel with His creatures, and just as He wishes that man shall not rule over man except for his good, so He would not want to force anyone to observe the commandments against his will nor to enter the Covenant at Sinai and the desert of Moab unless these commandments were accepted willingly....This is, indeed, somewhat difficult for the Jew living in Exile, who, from the moment he ceased to exist as a people in his own land, lost the cohesion of nationalism and thought that religion alone could serve as the bond and therefore that anyone who did not observe the religion was free of all obligations. There is, in fact, a natural force in humanity which ties even different peoples and members of different religions together into a nation; it is a vow of national

allegiance present in every people. God did not desire to rule by decree and commandment over Israel, but through a covenant with the people....

In any case, we know that the Jews were not obligated by the Torah and commandments, except through their own acceptance in a covenant and an oath....This is the true national bond which precedes peoplehood (*Malki BaKodesh*, Part C, pp. 80-81).

In this excerpt, nationalism was already conceived of as a principle which could stand independently, without religion; while Jewish religion as expressed in the Torah is inherently national since its essence is the covenant which places the people before God. It should be noted that nationalism in its pure form is based not on origin, but on the idea of the covenant, on the obligations which flow from the free choice of individuals vis-a-vis the people. In this sense, nationality is an expression of the will of individuals to be together and to establish a community that works together as one body. How, then, is the Torah unique as a national constitution? The answer to this question was given in the context of another discussion.

The nature and basis of the testimonies and laws and judgements which He did not give to the other nations, that is laws of which they were unaware, are five:

a) The peoples developed in their own lands and their laws and rules developed along with their way of life, so that they had no need for immutable, eternal laws of justice. Law and rules which come about naturally, in the course of life, evolve in response to living situations, not according to fixed laws of justice; laws which would perhaps be arrived at as well after thousands of years. Not so with us; we did not develop by ourselves into a people in our land; we were slaves to Pharaoh in Egypt and God took us out of Egypt to make us a people in the land which He promised to our forefathers; our development was not left to the evolutionary laws of nature. Instead, He gave us laws and rules that were complete, based on absolute laws of true justice which are not dependent on circumstances of time and life.

b) The testimonies and precepts are a memorial to the good which God did for us in taking us from slavery to freedom, to teach our children of the plight we were in and what we became afterwards through the loving-kindness of God.

c) The direction of the good that God did for us is Eretz Israel, which is the source of all the precepts and laws that the Lord our God commanded us.

d) The goal of all the laws is to make us God-fearing because awe prevents hastiness in the actions of man, so that he may avoid filling his desires without first assessing his deeds, without first considering whether his way is the path of righteousness or of evil...the laws of omission and commission accustom an individual to contemplate his actions and whether he should or should not persist in them. It would be best for us if all our lives we walked in the path of good and insured a remnant in Israel so that we would not be extinguished or lost among the many peoples who lived at the time when we were still slaves. Their memory has been forgotten, whereas we have survived to this day.

e) We must teach our children the notion that if we observe every commandment which God commanded us, we will justify our existence as a special people that dwells alone, a people chosen by God to live with honor in His land (*Torat HaHinukh*, p. 40).

These issues were summed up in an additional, brief sentence:

The reason for these laws is to relate our nationalism to our being a holy people with our God in His land which He promised to our forefathers...and these laws impose upon us an awe of God for our good so that we may remain a living people forever (*ibid.*, p. 61).

In other words, the uniqueness of the Torah as an ideal covenant of the people is its essential judicial eternity. Without a doubt, the religious aspect exists within it, but it is not separate from the national aspect which is revealed as the ideal totality of that same national covenant that is basically democratic.

In a philosophical context, Hirschensohn formulated the same idea in another way, influenced apparently by Rabbi Nachman Krochmal. Religion, he asserted, is the "soul" of the nation, i.e., the spiritual power uniting and activating the communal body which is composed of many individuals. The definition is based on Hirschensohn's psychology. In his opinion, the psyche is the unity of the spiritual powers that exists in all parts of the body and functions in all its limbs. But if the psyche is a spiritual essence connected to the body, the national psyche is *a priori* a common idea which unites the multitude of individuals and draws them to work together, not simply as a myriad of units but as one community. In this sense, then, religion is not just the "wealth" of a nation, it is the unifying idea. And just as there cannot be a body without a soul or a soul without a body, the Jewish nation cannot exist as a society without the religious component which is unique to it.

A detailed examination of these ideas will show that, at base, the possibility does exist of a certain distinction between nationality and religion, if not from the point of view of religion then at least from the point of view of nationality. Nationality, as the covenant of a people, is found in other nations, without the religious component. It would appear that such a distinction can also exist with regard to the Jewish people (a distinction already apparent in Hirschensohn's early essays) though this was difficult to realize in Exile, and therefore in Exile, Jewish nationality was identified with religion. Embodying within it both a blessing and a danger, Zionism, as a movement of modern nationalism, arose to revitalize this possibility.

Modern Jewish nationalism was born out of the Jew's desire to claim his full share of modern life. No longer satisfied to place his hopes in the future, he wanted a full life, both personally and nationally, in the here and now. This led to a desire to augment and expand areas of activity and creativity which Jews had avoided, or had been forcibly denied, in Exile, i.e., the introduction of a broad range of culture whose origin lay outside the scope of Jewry's self-expression. Initially, this appetite to take part in modern life did lead to assimilation. But assimilation could not produce a whole people, whereas from its inception, the national movement sought to restore to the Jewish people the fullness of sovereignty. Rabbi Kook, who was aware of this fact no less than Hirschensohn, approached it with concepts drawn from the ancient heritage of Jewish thought. For him, modern nationalism had arisen only to return to the Jewish people what had originally been taken from them by force, now seen outside Jewry's parameters because of the limitations of Exile. There is no positive development in the world which is not also rooted in Jewish sources. Jews who are fervently drawn to positive areas which they find in the cultures of other nations are, in fact, only seeking to restore to Judaism what it once had and was taken from it, although they themselves do not know this. Rabbi Kook saw himself as having a greater perspective: he knew that what a secular nationalist would see as borrowing from a foreign culture in the service of expanding national creativity was nothing less than the return of the scattered remnants of Judaism to itself.

Hirschensohn did not need this dialectic; the historical facts lay before him in unqualified simplicity. A movement had arisen among the people which was seeking to expand the precincts of national life with material borrowed from the environing peoples. Who could fault that? Although he knew the risks involved in aspiring to a full modern life, Hirschensohn's response was very clear: it was certainly a positive development. It was also correct from the *halakhic* aspect. Since the Torah relates to the life of the people and its totality, it should accept a positive addition to national life, even if the source is an external one.[2] But the duality which is created if such a determination is reached is impossible to ignore, at least as long as the Torah, in its commandments and *halakhah*, has not adjusted to the new development. This is even truer when large segments of the people worked to incorporate external sources without considering themselves bound by the Torah. In other words, the new Jewish nationalism created a clear-cut phenomenon of Jewish nationality which existed independently and this situation demanded that Torah scholars relate to it as it was perceived by those who created it.

At this point an interesting development began to occur in Hirschensohn's nationalist thinking. If at first he thought that it was possible to integrate the principles of modern nationalism within the broad scope of a religious national revival which sought to preserve the identity between nationality and religion, he later came to the conclusion that there was no escape from the admission of a duality of principles which were similar but not identical. Paradoxically, his willingness to change his initial conclusion stemmed from his loyalty to that same concept, at least as an ideal vision of the future. The extent of the dilemma before him was that if a strict identity between nationality and Jewish religion was maintained, at the very least it would mean giving up on a large part of the Jewish people. If the Torah were to remain the Torah of the Jewish people, it had to come to terms with the fact that part of the Jewish people had removed themselves from its authority.

Believing as he did, in the early period, that it was possible to subsume the duality into a unity, Hirschensohn posited that the Jewish people would revive its national life in its land according to the Torah. Unity would thus be reinstated. Of course, this meant a willingness to be daring concerning *halakhah*. In principle, this was possible: the Torah is a guide to life and there was no necessity for a split between it and the people. Therefore, he expected, as did Rabbi Yitzhak Yaacov Reines and Rabbi Kook, that in the end the secular national movement would become a movement for a return to Torah Judaism. He did not base this expectation on predictions in the mystic lore and the advent of the Messiah, or on their meta-national and meta-historical aspects. His expectations were based on historical factors in what he saw as a historical process. The majority of the people were faithful to the Torah. If the majority of the people who were faithful to the Torah identified with Zionism, and if *halakhic* creativity were renewed, then national life in Eretz Israel would be established on *halakhic* principles; the secular sector would accommodate to the majority and would certainly see the truth of the Torah.[3] Since this expectation was based on historical observation and on an assessment of historical factors, it is not surprising that a change occurred in Hirschensohn's views as a result of his experiences of Jewish life in America.

And your eminence should know that the thoughts which you had concerning nationalism and religion were my thoughts 45 years ago; I have worked in conformity with this idea all my life on the Zionist project, which, with God's help, I was active in establishing although I was not one of the major founders. It was with this idea that I became a member of Mizrahi, at its inception, through my dear friend, the late Rabbi Reines, of blessed memory. That was before I came to know the Jewish Exile well. I thought [all Jews] were like the people in Eretz Israel, or in Poland and Lithuania, and sinners I thought to be a minority as "the dregs of the vineyard of Judea," but when I came to America and got to know my fellow Jews from other parts of the world, I saw the decadence that Hosea saw, and I felt that this was not a worthless minority but a large majority of our own brothers. It is our obligation to have mercy on the remnant of Israel, or better said, to have mercy on them and deal charitably with them when they take pity on us with their material contributions. Whoever loves

13

his people and his religion must think so (*Malki BaKodesh*, Sec. 10, pp. 115-116).

This position was motivated by love for the Jewish people and by compassionate "spirituality"; and it was finely mannered in an expression meant for the God-fearing rabbi to whom the letter was sent. In actuality, the precision of Hirschensohn's words in other contexts (to which we shall return below) demonstrates that he recognized that there were differences in the phenomenon of non-observant Jews; he could relate to nationalist Jews whose rejection of the Torah was a sincere expression of their reasoned outlook on life, a view which was difficult to change and whose claims could not be facilely dismissed. What conclusions came out of his experience? The answer is not a negation of the basic principles he had previously held, but their reapplication. Jewish religion is national and cannot be otherwise, but Jewish nationality can exist separately from religion and, in essence, the doctrine of nationalism accepts religion, if only critically and from an ability to struggle with it in order to change the reality.

I also belong to Mizrahi, but not because I think that Jewish nationalism is its religion. This is something in which most religious people, and Mizrahi Zionists, are mistaken. The truth is that the Jewish religion is a national religion, but there is no Jewish nationalism except for religious nationalism. Religion is only one of the conditions of the life of a people; it preceded the people and helps its moral progress and enhances it through spiritual enrichment, but it is not nationality, just as wealth is not life, even though it sustains and brings life. Have we not seen that at a time when the majority of the Jewish people worshipped idols and honored other gods that the prophets castigated them; nonetheless, they called them the people of God....All this shows clearly that Jewish nationalism is not dependent on its religion; when Israel sinned it was called an iniquitous people, and when it ameliorated its ways it was called a holy people; throughout they remained children dear to their God. No sin in the world can erase the nationality of a person. Of course, we must belong to Mizrahi, not because Jewish nationalism is only religion, but the opposite, because the Jewish religion is entirely national. Every religious person should belong to Mizrahi in order to strengthen religion and to act as a counter-weight to secular nationalists who do not know how to recognize the value of religion and, knowingly or unknowingly, will cause its disintegration. Each religious person must stand in the breach with whatever strength he has on behalf of religion.

This strength is found now only within Mizrahi ideology because those religious circles who oppose nationalism are not to be considered supporters of the Jewish religion, even if they observe all the commandments in all their details. The national content in each and every commandment is patently apparent to the unprejudiced eye...when our sages spoke of "pious idol worshippers" their allusion was to religious persons who oppose Jewish nationalism....Such is the truth of their character because delusion which opposes the Torah and its spirit is idol worship, while the spirit of the Torah is Jewish nationalism (*Malki BaKodesh*, Sec. 4, pp. 244-247).

Hirschensohn was insistent and consistent. If religiosity which is not nationalist is not really Judaism, then Jewish nationalism, even if it not religious, nonetheless fulfills the national basis of religion. This does not mean that Hirschensohn was prepared to cede religious obligations, even on the part of the nationalist Jew who was not religious. The claim remains valid due to the unique nature of Jewish nationality which could not sustain itself for long and would be completely empty of content if it did not maintain a religious component.

To further understand this, it is useful to preface what is said in the continuation of this letter, with several sentences from another letter, part of which was quoted above:

The religious Jew can say about a Jew who transgresses — even a heretical or idol-worshipping Jew, so long as he has not left the community, changed his nationality or given up his religion in order to assimilate among the gentiles — the religious Jew can say, though he has transgressed still he is a Jew; this is not because religion is not part of nationality, but because the Jewish religion is a national asset, and whoever negates a single point of Jewish religion robs Jewish nationality and impoverishes it, just as someone who negates the entire Jewish religion empties Jewish nationalism. A national Jew, whether he is religious or a non-believer, should pity such an unfortunate person and try to instill in him our spirit of religion, not denigrate him or cast him out of the Jewish people (*ibid.*, Sec. 6, pp. 115-116).

In other words, non-religious nationalism is still nationalism, although it is empty of content "...because for a religious Jew, empty nationalism is like a body without a soul, a person as good as dead. Someone poor in spirit is also dead" (*ibid.*).
The conclusion drawn from the continuation of the previous letter thus becomes clear.

Indeed, the secular nationalist should not say to the religious person: You, as a religious person, are correct to strengthen religion in your midst, to teach ethics and faith just as the Prophets did; but you have no right to involve religion in politics as an arm of Zionism and to force a decision on all Zionists to be religious. I would answer him: You are wrong, secularist, you are wrong! (*ibid.*, Sec. 4, pp. 244-247).

There are two nationalist reasons for this decision. The first is that our return to our land at this time is not the return of conquerors but the return of inheritors, and the right of our inheritance to Eretz Israel is religious. The second reason is that the bond between the Jews in Exile and Jews in Eretz Israel can only be a religious bond, for

Zionism will undoubtedly bring life to the Jewish people but it will not bring it eternity...for eternity for us is only in the Torah....[Therefore] we must try with all our might to magnify and glorify the Torah, teach ethics, religion and unswerving faith and proceed moderately until we succeed so that Eretz Israel exists for the Jewish people according to the Torah, and the Torah guides the Jewish people in Eretz Israel (*ibid.*).

Thus the discussion comes full circle, and there is recognition of a Jewish nationality which is not religious. What is it based on? Part of the answer is already clear from the previous discussion: a nationalist is someone who does not remove himself from the community or has not uprooted himself from the covenant of the people which, for Hirschensohn, is the essential principle of nationality.

His attitude toward those who convert to another religion is based on this assumption. The convert excludes himself from anything Jewish not because he worships idols, but because he has overstepped the border of Jewish nationality. Conversion is the most radical step toward assimilation because it is entry into another communal framework and entails complete identification with the principal cultural characteristics of another nation. But someone who has not converted and has not assimilated in any other way, who binds his fate to that of the Jewish people, is a nationalist Jew, and he is such according to the Torah as well. Hirschensohn added two considerations to this: faithfulness to the Hebrew language and faithfulness to Eretz Israel. These two obligatory loyalties emanate from the Torah. There is no true knowledge of Torah without Hebrew, and one cannot carry out all its commandments outside Eretz Israel. Language and country are the principles of the separate existence of the nation. Here again, there are national values to which religion is inseparably bound. The individual who is faithful to them — even if he does not live according to the Torah — is within the national covenant.

What, then, should the proper attitude be toward the secular nationalist Jewish sector? One answer is found in the public arena and another on the personal plane. At the public level, Hirschensohn was prepared for a hard struggle which could not be avoided once the Jewish state was established in Eretz Israel. The religious sector would insist that the state be run according to *halakhah* and that the religious commandments be upheld. The secular sector would place emphasis on national values as such, and on fortifying the political framework of the nation. If it were prepared for in advance, the struggle could be a fruitful one. If the religious sector were ready with appropriate *halakhic* solutions regarding the administration of a modern state on its own soil and an independent national life, and if, even in the era leading to the establishment of the state no legal separation was created between the religious and secular sectors, but the rulings of *halakhah* were to apply in the domain of civil life — then it would be a "peaceful war" conducted in the spirit of the Prophets, and there was a chance that it would succeed. *Malki BaKodesh* was written to meet this situation.[4]

On the personal plane, Hirschensohn distinguished between nationalists who arrived at their anti-religious position through sincere reasoning — he respected them and wanted to work with

17

them in the upbuilding of the land — in contrast to those whose attitude was a reflection of disparagement and irresponsibility. People who mocked religion were evil doers; nonetheless, one should not respond to them in kind unless their distortions were being spread in public, nor should they be publicly embarrassed. A way should be found to cooperate with them in the nationalist arena for it was necessary that everyone work toward building the national future. The main determinant in these issues was a measure of benevolence at the national level; the measure of judgment would be drawn only concerning the individual who had knowingly assimilated or someone who openly and intentionally insulted the sacred institution of the Torah.[5]

Hirschensohn's love of the Jewish people, which is expressed, as will be seen below, in his *halakhic* outlook, expanded to include love of one's fellow-man in its broadest sense. His faithfulness to Jewish nationalism was at one with the ideal of a united humanity. It is important to emphasize that Hirschensohn conceived of nationalism in its democratic aspect, a conceptualization that substantiates the difference between nationality and nationalism. In an article printed in *HaMisdarona*, in 1897,[6] Hirschensohn fiercely rejected European nationalism. Typical of his attitude was the feeling of pride which he expressed in an essay on the involvement of Jews in the movements for national and social liberation of the people in whose midst they lived. Although such involvement took Jews away from activity on behalf of their own people, Hirschensohn did not see this as evidence of assimilation; on the contrary, it was the mark of a supreme Torah quality: dedication to an ethical goal on behalf of humanity. In his opinion, it was testimony to the axiom that Jews always contributed more to their surroundings than they received from them, which was as it should be.

For this wise and clever nation is not closed up in the small circle of its own nationalism alone, but the wider world is also close to its heart. If, in a national sense, every Jew is to be faithful to his people, then this Jewish national identity calls for filling the world with a love of humanity that is as the love of God; and nation shall not life up sword against nation, neither shall they learn of war any more (*Malki BaKodesh*, Sec. 3, p. 47).

These notions took on added relevancy when Hirschensohn applied them to issues which involved relationships between the Jewish people and other peoples; to begin with, the issue of the right to Eretz Israel. Hirschensohn refers to this in his book, *Nimukei Rashi,* in a discussion on the interpretation of the first passage in Genesis. Of special interest is his statement that Rashi's response to the ostensible accusation made by the gentiles that the Jewish people had stolen the land of the seven Canaanite nations, is not a response to the gentiles but a response to the ethical sensitivity which is typical of Jews. The gentiles, in fact, recognized the right of conquest, not only in the past but also in the present. If there is a fear of criticism directed toward the Jews, it is that the land was conquered from us by others, and that we have not reconquered it. But here there is a difficulty

...which rises essentially from out of the life of the people, and therefore its resolution must come from within the life of the people; Rashi found that, by its very nature, the Jewish people was exquisitely sensitive to the opinion of the other nations, and could not withstand the apparent accusations of gentiles saying, you are robbers in that you conquered the land of the seven nations. They could not accept the promise "And I will bring you into the land which I swore to give to Abraham, to Isaac and to Jacob; I will give it to you as a possession." If the right to it was not clear to them, and if the One who promised this was considered by them as the One who promised "We shall find every precious thing, we shall fill our houses with the spoils" (Proverbs 1:13), no Jew could accept such a promise unless the justice of it was clear to him (*Nimukei Rashi*, p. 2,1).

Hirschensohn, of course, accepted Rashi's answer which is rooted in the notion that God is sovereign over the world, but he saw a need to broaden the scope. According to the law of nations, the conquest of a land implies ownership in the political sense. But conquest does not justify confiscating right of private ownership from the people conquered on their own soil. In Hirschensohn's opinion, the prerogative to settle the land, not only hold it politically, is a right that is rooted in the inheritance of the forefathers. This is the claim to Eretz Israel.

Related to this issue is the issue of a war of conquest and the commandment to destroy the inhabitants of the land. Hirschensohn stated as a *halakhic* ruling that a holy war binds Jews only to the boundaries of their forefathers possessions, and not to the boundaries of the Divine promise;[7] even this would apply only to a given political and military situation.[8] The commandments of destruction, Hirschensohn saw as a specific command which, for several reasons, was unavoidable historically.

> But when the kingdom of Israel was strengthened by David and Solomon and they no longer had any fear, and the war of conquest was completely over, there was no need to kill people wantonly; it was forbidden to spill innocent blood. Thus David and Solomon did not kill them but exacted taxes and put them into servitude. The commandment to conquer Eretz Israel continued for generations...but there was no duty that none should be left alive, and not only was this not obligatory but it was forbidden to trespass international laws laid down in the convention of nations on how to conduct oneself in war. God forbid that the Jews should be considered among the nations as wild murderers who act against international conventions and the laws of civilization (*Eileh Divrei HaBrit*, Vol. 1, p. 70).

The fact that "international conventions" applied to the Jewish people from the aspect of an absolute, binding covenant was of great concern to Hirschensohn (we shall return to this question in a chapter devoted to the democratic-*halakhic* idea in his theories). There is no doubt that Hirschensohn was convinced of the right of the Jewish people to the land of its forefathers, in its entirety; indeed, he was an energetic opponent of the concession made by the Executive of the World Zionist Organization which relinquished the inclusion of Transjordan within the borders of the national homeland.[9] He nonetheless insisted, with the same degree of forcefulness, that international laws of justice and ethics be observed in the process of settlement, and that democratic procedures be maintained with regard to non-Jewish inhabitants of Eretz Israel.

A third issue, the attitude of *halakhah* towards non-Jews in general, expands on this last statement. Hirschensohn came to the fervent determination that all of the ethical commandments which the Torah imposes on a Jew relate to every individual, regardless of who he may be, and that in this respect the Torah does not discriminate positively in favor of the Jew. The path of justice and charity to which the Torah commands us guides our behavior toward all men; if there are some areas in which the obligation of a Jew is greater, these are areas of religious obligations which go beyond what is required by law and justice in man's relationship to his fellow-man.[10] Hirschensohn took the position that a Jew who participates as a judge in a non-Jewish trial must act according to the severity of *halakhah* in all matters concerning the trial, even if the law of country is not as severe as that of *halakhah*. In the concept of Torah, wherever justice is concerned, it is the concern of all people, and the Jew must act accordingly in his relationship with every person because he is a human being.[11] Hirschensohn believed that the Torah could be a guide for achieving the best solutions to the social problems which arise in a modern state, and that a Jewish state which was guided by *halakhah* in all matters concerning relationships between man and his fellow-man, would indeed be a light unto the nations.

Notes

1. See *Eleh Divrei HaBrit*, Sec. A, Ch. A.
2. This is the direction Hirschensohn takes in the majority of his articles in *HaMisdarona*; for example: "Hesdarim Ba'Halakhah V'Hokhmot HaTzionit," in Vol. 2.
3. See *Malki BaKodesh*, Sec. 7, pp. 115-116.
4. *Ibid.*, p. 123.
5. *Ibid.*, Sec. 2, response to the third question.
6. See "The Bible and Aggada," *HaMisdarona*, Vol. 2.
7. See *Eileh Divrei HaBrit*, Sec. 1, Ch. 1.
8. *Ibid.*, Sec. 3, Ch. 16.
9. *Op. cit.*, Sec. A, Ch. 1.
10. See *Sefer Torat HaHinukh HaYisraeli*, Article 4, Ch. 2, Par. 4.
11. See *Malki BaKodesh*, Sec. 2, response to the fourth question.

Chapter 3

THE RELATIONSHIP TO SECULAR CULTURE

Although the term "secular" often appears in Hirschensohn's writings, nowhere is there a definition of either secularism as a phenomenon or of secular culture. There is no doubt, however, that the term secular refers to a Jew who, knowingly, does not observe the Torah and its commandments. It was characteristic of Hirschensohn that his negative attitude toward this aspect of secularism did not apply to the positive cultural expressions developed by secularists in areas other than religion, even when some of these expressions appeared to deny basic principles of the Torah. (Here, too, there is an effort to understand the secular Jew and bring him closer to religion.)

If this is Hirschensohn's basic stance, then he perceives these cultural expressions in the same light as they were presented by those who advocated them: as manifestations of human progress. His admission of human cultural progress does not, however, negate his belief in the authority of the Torah or the absolute value of its beliefs and commandments. In this, he again follows Maimonides in accepting *a priori* that there is no possibility for a contradiction between Torah and that which is best in the achievements of the human spirit. Whatever appears to be a denial of Torah precepts is seen as a challenge to be met by an openness to truth and complete faith in the Torah. Ultimately, those expressions which were created outside the province of religion will find their place within its sweep because Jewish religion is intended to encompass the fullness of life. Thus, from the religious view, secular manifestations are not, in essence, secular; they can be an inseparable part of religious culture without undermining its foundations or perverting its principles.[1] This is, of course, a general formula; the test lies in its detailed application. The original sense of the formula becomes manifest when it is applied: that is, the daring to confront precisely those topics which, from a religious perspective, appear most dangerous. Any issue in which a secular cultural achievement seems to undermine conventional religious attitudes ought to be regarded as a primary challenge. It is in these issues that the precise limits of human comprehesion can be seen, and it is here that the distinction can be made between a genuine cultural achievement, and an illusory one that is based on error or a fanciful flight that transcends the bounds of human intellect.

Hirschensohn follows Maimonides in this as well, except that the "battlegrounds" have changed. The emphasis is no longer on philosophy. Still, in his affinity to Spinoza on this point, Hirschensohn is true to his own approach: he clearly sees in Spinoza the person who laid the foundation for a critical outlook toward religion in general, and toward Judaism in particular. Hirschensohn believed that Spinoza made a fatal error; nonetheless, he should certainly not be seen as either an apostate or a heretic. Aware of the deep religious feelings that pulsated within Spinoza and his efforts to apply a dimension of sanctity to what he mistakenly believed to be God, Hirschensohn stated categorically that as Spinoza wrote in accordance with his own best understanding, it was the truth in his eyes. Consequently, he ought not be considered a transgressor. An error is not a sin; indeed, if the error was made out of a zealousness for the truth and from total conviction, it even has merit.[2] That is to say, Spinoza's thought needed to be confronted by critical, germane thinking which would indicate his error. This is the crucial point which separates Hirschensohn's approach from that of the Orthodox position. For every matter in which Orthodoxy shies away from a substantive encounter and erects barriers to thought, Hirschensohn calls for a daring break-through. A pertinent examination will reveal the truth of the Torah, even if that truth turns out to be different from what was previously thought.

As stated, the issues are relevant to the philosophical realm, as well, but the major "battlegrounds" are in other areas of creativity. Where does Hirschensohn see those areas of human progress that are contemporaneous to his time? In his writings, the salient areas are progress in the natural sciences which advanced our knowledge of cosmology, the emergence and structure of the world, the development of life, the structure of matter and of psychology; progress in the humanities, especially in historical research which uncovered in great detail the history of ancient nations, including that of ancient Israel; social progress which heightened an awareness of slavery and exploitation and which raised the issue of social justice to the extent that it could no longer be ignored; political progress as expressed in the spread of democracy as the most perfect and just political system; and finally, the significant progress made in understanding the concept of truth, even in the realm of theology. Indeed, the principle of God's incorporeality and the rejection of pagan mythology are now accepted throughout enlightened humanity. All of this is indicative of the extent of progress which has been made by general culture.

Hirschensohn did not, however, appear to suffer from the enthusiastically accepted illusion that progress was the only yardstick for judging the worth of modern human culture, of even the most enlightened nations. The experience of World War I left a lasting impression on him, and he knew very well that headway, in the sense of a spreading awareness of certain moral conventions in societal life and in the state, did not really constitute moral advancement.[3] His was not the unbridled, optimistic belief in progress of the nineteenth century. Hirschensohn did believe that there was definite progress in certain defined areas of spiritual creativity. However, from the standpoint of Torah, problems do arise, sometimes even difficult problems, and in each one of these areas.

Progress in the natural sciences raises doubts concerning views about Creation which are accepted in the religious literature, including views which, at least initially, appear to be fundamental to belief. If truth be told, Hirschensohn did not attach great importance to these dilemmas. To his mind, the task of reconciling scientific conclusions (even Darwin's theory of the Origin of the Species) with belief in the Torah was relatively easy: the Torah only hinted at scientific truths; rather than knowing everything in advance, the task of human beings is to seek wisdom. Thus scientific truth was revealed gradually and never to its fullest extent. Ex post facto, one might recognize, in a passage of Torah, the intimation of a scientific truth that had just been proven but even in such cases it would be wiser not to examine these intimations too closely since that was not the intent of the Torah. The basic principle is that the world was created, and that all creatures, including those whose perfection involved a lengthy period of development — such as human beings — were created in the beginning in the sense that their eventual evolvement, even their final form, was already determined at the time of Creation.[4]

Hirschensohn was more concerned with the implications of scientific and technological progress and the moral, religious and educational questions that such progress raised in its application to a way of life. Ought *halakhah* permit autopsies which were vital to medical progress? Should *halakhah* allow the use of electrical devices on Shabbat when in reality to avoid doing so in the future would be almost impossible? Above all, how could the conflict be solved between the demands of Torah education which, as traditionally understood, requires total dedication, and scientific and technological education and specialization which also require serious application of time and effort?

Advances in historical research raised a theoretical question of principle along with a specific question of even greater gravity and peril. The question of principle had to do with whether the notion of historical progress could be reconciled with the concept of the Torah's authority, while the particular question was concerned with how to relate to the results of historical criticism and philological research into Holy Scripture. In view of the dangers involved, should such research be permitted?

Progress in the societal realm has placed the question of social justice on the *halakhic* agenda, especially in employer-employee relations. Hirschensohn believed that in this area the Torah had a decided advantage, for it could enlighten from out of its own inner light. But here there is a problem, for what the Torah has to teach on this topic was hidden and would continue to remain so unless a concerted effort was made to apply the principles of *halakhah* to solving the social problems of modern life. A consciousness of social equality raises additional questions which border on the political realm, one of the most important being women's status according to *halakhah*, as well as social relationships between Jews and Gentiles, a matter alluded to earlier.

In the area of political progress, the fact that democracy in the modern era has been enshrined as the political ideal of most nations is undoubtedly a manifestation of progress. The problem arises, however, as to whether the Torah view, as crystallized in *halakhah*, allows for a democratic Jewish state? What is the nature of *halakhic* democracy? This is the key question concerning the Jewish state and its institutions, with many other queries that derive from it (such as the status of women and attitudes toward non-Jews and the civil courts). These are fundamental matters which pertain, first of all, to the realization of Zionism in the Land of Israel, but are also relevant to Jewish life in the diaspora, especially in those countries which extrapolated from their democratic principles an attitude of full civic equality for the Jews.

Finally, there is the issue of progress as a world view and way of thought as evidenced in the decline of the value of myth and the triumph of cognitive judgment in the realm of religion. This progress in world consciousness raises a question about ancient elements which relate to ritual. True, these elements have no current validity, but their validity may be renewed with the renewal of a Jewish dominion. In sharp, practical terms, how are we to relate to the Temple Mount in the reborn Jewish state? In particular, what will our attitude be to sacrifices? What are the implications of prayer for the renewal of the Temple service?

These are the main topics with which Hirschensohn dealt in his essays. It is thus clear that in his relationship to secularism, Hirschensohn was concerned with the practical application of those problematics which are inherent in a positive view of modern Jewish nationalism. His aspiration was to work toward finding positive solutions to all these issues.

Notes

1. See Note 1 of the previous chapter.
2. See *Musagei Shav V'HaEmet*, pp. 115-118.
3. See his letter to Rabbi Abraham Isaac HaCohen Kook, *Malki BaKodesh*, Ch. 4.
4. See *Eilah Divrei HaBrit*, Part II, Ch. 4.

Chapter 4

THE TEMPTATION OF MATERIALISM

Though he was not unaware of its pitfalls, Haim Hirschensohn had a positive regard for the higher aspects of secular culture. This acceptance did not, however, apply to its more ignoble features, especially when these communicated themselves in the temptations of a materialistic lifestyle. While a sociological analysis of this process is not a part of his work, the phenomena are clearly described in the course of his *halakhic* deliberations. His starting point was an awareness of objective difficulties. Integration into European culture, and its spiritual manifestations, had already given rise to complications at the educational level which had a direct bearing on everyday life. The Torah scholar who devoted every moment to study was to become an increasingly rare creature, and scholarly bourgeoisie of the classic model could no longer persevere in their part-time studies. Individuals who had previously occupied themselves exclusively in Torah now had to expend much time on other studies as well. Yet the knowledge of Torah as a widespread phenomenon among the people, as distinguished from the preserve of an elite, had been the underlying assumption for the existence of a Jewish way of life.[1]

This vicissitude was still in the area of the higher challenge; the common challenge, however, was the outcome of an objective difficulty of a different sort. In the open society which Rabbi Haim Hirschensohn encountered in the United States, a Jew's livlihood derived increasingly from the customs and institutions of non-Jewish society. The Jew could no longer retain isolated Jewish life forms in accordance with *halakhah*'s strictures without encountering almost insurmountable hardships. An uncompromising observance of *halakhah* would seriously compromise his livlihood. This applied particularly to the Jewish masses. A Jewish storeowner who closed his business on Saturday was likely to lose customers; a Jewish laborer who stayed away from work on the Sabbath could be fired.

These were objective constraints that could be viewed as coercive and hence merited some forbearance from the strict letter of the law, if only as a temporary measure. Nonetheless, Rabbi Hirschensohn knew full well that defining these difficulties as "coercion" was not uncomplicated. Nor was the predicament solely a *halakhic*-formalistic one, but rather a substantively psychological one. For compulsion is measured by subjectivity. It very much depends on what an individual regards as a limitation with which he cannot live. Where does one draw the line between an absolute existential requirement and the pursuit of profits and economic success for their own sake?[2]

In other words, the economic and social integration of Jews in their environment involves both the cause and effect of their material aspirations. Commitment and devotion to a Torah way of life and its precepts is weakened in the face of the pursuit of material advancement. Even when the loosening of bonds begins from objective difficulties, it cannot but spread to other areas. Whatever chafes because it is inconvenient, whether it is perceived as a limitation, or as being outlandish in the new environment, is gradually abandoned. Consequently, materialism sweeps everything connected with Torah observance before it, according to a criterion of material success, on one hand, and a desire for convenience, on the other.

It bears noting that in Hirschensohn's view this phenomenon affects all Jews. It does not apply solely to Jews who overtly intend to unburden themselves of the commandments but to followers of the Orthodox camp as well, giving rise to a *halakhic* question: how is one to relate to members of Mizrahi who do not observe the Sabbath according to *halakhah*?[3] In essence, a way of life whose motive force is material success constitutes an obstacle and is a competitor to a Torah observant way of life. Its secularity does not consist of a principled denial of the religion, its beliefs and values, but is an absolute erosion of the ways and arrangements of religion.

On the ideological plane this presents one problem, but in praxis, it is reflected in a variety of processes and calls for a confrontation with a whole series of difficulties. These include a slackening of the communal structure, a waning authority on the part of rabbis and Torah scholars, and the fragmentation of the Jewish public, particularly the isolation of those who wish to fortify their beliefs against the sweeping tide. Conflicts and disorientation abound precisely at a time when unity is called for. Worst of all, the underpinnings of education for the young have been flattened. Jewish education is enabled only when the family discharges its responsibilities, but even the little that parents would wish to convey cannot be transmitted in a Jewish home devoid of Torah study and observance of the *mitzvot*. Consequently, parents expect the school to import to their children that which they themselves no longer perform. The outcome is that whereas the parents place religious observance at a distance, whether out of actual compulsion or out of a desire to appear coerced, the children distance themselves due to ignorance and spiritual disinterest.[4]

Haim Hirschensohn realized that a similar process was afoot in Israel. Yet it would appear that he was less anxious about it because in Israel, at least, national commitments were maintained. The secular community in Israel also worked toward the redemption of the people with great devotion. This was not the case in the Golah.

Notes

1. See the opening article in *Misdarona*, as well as *Torat HaHinukh HaYisraeli*, Article III.
2. See *Malki BaKodesh*, Part II, the response to Question 3, which deals with people who desecrate the Sabbath in the belief that they are forced to work in order to stay alive.
3. *Op. cit.*
4. See *Torat HaHinukh HaYisraeli*, Article III, Ch. ii, Par. 7.

Chapter 5

TORAH AND LIFE

There is a basic assumption in Haim Hirschensohn's proposed solutions which is anchored in his national-religious perception and which determines his position on all the issues previously discussed. If the Torah of Israel is essentially national, and if the religion is "the wealth" of Jewish national life or the "idea" uniting that life, then one is obliged, as far as both the essence of Torah and the national interest are concerned, to prevent a split between the Torah (or the religion) and national life in its broadest sense. If the Torah ceased to guide every aspect of the nation's life, it would no longer fulfill its original intention. Hirschensohn viewed that possibility as a danger which could destroy the distinctive feature of the Jewish religion and, needless to say, if that happened, Jewish nationality would lose first its inner richness and then its unifying character.

Thus, in principle, the Torah should relate to national life in its fullest sense, dealing with each problem that arises in order to find a positive solution for it from a national standpoint. What is good for the nation as such must find its proper place in a way of life guided by *halakhah*. It is precisely because they derive from the essence of Torah that the solutions ought to be sought out. Such a course of action, however, is by no means certain. It demands a constant spiritual effort because each of the areas of activity involved — religion and *halakhah*, and nationalism — are the face of different aggregates which tend to grow widely disparate: religion and *halakhah* are intrinsically conservative, while nationalism grapples with new and dynamic situations. The question, therefore, of "what is Torah," can never have a final, unalterable answer because Torah must be renewed in each generation according to prevailing circumstances. This would permit the nation to live according to the Torah rather than contending with *halakhic* rulings made for circumstances no longer relevant and which cannot therefore provide a basis for present-day life.

Earlier, during his *Misdarona* period, Hirschensohn emphatically stressed this idea which he considered of particular importance, in his article, "Which is Mishnah?" His answer was that the Mishnah went beyond the narrow letter of the law.

Its purpose is to concisely interpret most *halakhic* issues, doubts and disagreements and to encompass all the laws of the Torah. This will enable the sages of each generation to plough when it is time to plough, to plant when the time comes to plant, and to reap when it is time to reap so that the public is not unduly burdened by doubt and sophistry which take up too much time before a ruling is made telling the people what they should do in order to live according to the Torah. As has been said, "interpretations of the Torah will one day be forgotten by Israel"; this raises a difficulty because it is also written: "And it will not be forgotten!" Thus one is bound to conclude that there are no absolutely final *halakhic* rulings. The purpose of the Mishnah is then to enable an ongoing interpretation, and this way it becomes a pillar of support for Israeli national life....After this introduction we may understand why the question of "which is Mishnah" is so important. It is indeed important for each generation because each generation contributes to the increased *halakhic* knowledge, and it becomes a duty to find out what is the meaning of the Mishnah for this specific generation. But in our generation it is particularly important, while no one tries to resolve it. Thus, every individual feels that his spiritual life depends on this question: "Which is Mishnah?" (*Hamisdarona*, Vol. 2, p. 262).

The issue of "which is Mishnah" has, indeed, become much more crucial in our generation. At the conclusion of the first part of his book, *Malki BaKodesh*, Hirschensohn wrote that his generation had experienced more change in a few years than previous generations had in hundreds of years, and that the pace would yet accelerate. *Halakhic* thought, however, trailed far behind, and the gap between life and Torah had grown wider and wider. Even more disturbing was the resulting generational gap which could be overcome if only *halakhah* would deal head-on with the changing reality and not persist in refusing to acknowledge the positive aspects of national life.

Regarding the Torah as national in its essence should not be seen as a statement that the Torah and nationalism are in fact identical, but rather as a demand that the Torah can ideally fulfill. A dichotomy could evolve between the Torah and life, but even under conditions of exceptionally quick and extreme change this need not happen. By its very nature, the Torah is adaptable and, in principle, there is no situation for which a positive solution cannot be found according to *halakhah* — so long as its interpreters, the sages of Israel, show an understanding and readiness to do so. As a national religion, the Torah of Israel is not "cut" along dogmatic lines. It is open to a changing reality and continues to develop from generation to generation.

This concept, of course, is not new as even the most exacting of the ultra-Orthodox would concur. The crucial question now is the way in which the principle is to be interpreted: 1) from the aspect of understanding the nature and workings of the process and its application, and 2) from the aspect of willingness and daring to actually employ it. In both instances, Hirschensohn's originality is apparent. He dared to use the principle extensively and consistently in dealing with essential issues, and he had the courage to interpret the nature and workings of the process in a way different from that of the Orthodox or the Reform.

It would appear that the conflict between Hirschensohn and the Orthodox focuses on three assumptions that he developed and about which he was consistent.

The kind of religion that was allotted to other peoples cannot inhere for a people like Israel whose nationhood is bound up with its religion as a flame is joined to its coals. Nor under any circumstances could the nation, in its tribulations through fire and water, have continued to exist if not for the Talmud and the logic of *halakhah* which He gave to His people to light up their path in all the circumstances of life, and to explicate matters involving the people's two pillars — religion and nationhood — which are occasionally so contesting that it would seem they could not stand together were it not for this logic which has the potential of extricating the people from out of the maze *(Malki BaKodesh*, Vol. 1, p. 20).

The emphasis above is on the phrase, "Talmud and logic of *halakhah*." What did this phrase mean for Hirschensohn? The answer is in the following passage where he deals with a practical issue.

35

The words of the Torah — "whose ways are pleasant and whose paths are peace" — contain nothing which contradicts genuine civilization or which would ever requires us to do anything contrary to reason....True, we must base ourselves on the Torah and its *mitzvot* and reflect upon them according to the methods of "our sages, blessed be their memory," as well as understand their words according to the objectives toward which they aspired when they interpreted the *mitzvot* — then we shall see that they loved truth and peace....For only the Zaddokites and, later, the Karaites — who did not fathom the inner meaning of Scripture and the purpose of Torah and the aspirations of our sages — were discomfited by political life and thought it incompatible with what was of the essence for them and therefore that it contradicted the Torah; they raised religion above political life, and in their self-justification set themselves apart like the Essenes in Second Temple times, and like the Karaites in Jerusalem at the end of the Gaonic period (*Malki BaKodesh*, Vol. 1, p. 21-22).

Halakhic logic is not merely a formal-legal logic; it also has an aspect of straightforward reasoning by its adjudicators whose criteria is whatever they regard as flowing from the knowledge of the true and the good. Thus, in order to arrive at a *halakhic* ruling, adjudicators should not base their decisions only on the dry letter of the law, but delve into "the soul of Scripture" to uncover the ethical, social and religio-spiritual considerations upon which each former ruling was based. In this way their rulings would be established on a living religio-ethical spirit. One should, therefore, endeavor to uncover the internal motives for why the early adjudicators ruled as they did.

Not for a moment did Hirschensohn believe those rulings contrary to reason and morality. Sufficient precedent, he felt, could be found in *halakhah* for every decision which was required and had to be made in accordance with contemporary reason and morality. In the following incisive passage from a polemical letter to Rabbi Kook, his intention is clear.

I do not believe that everything I am struggling for should remain unchanged from a moral standpoint. I know that from a true, moral standpoint much needs to be changed and in my book, *Musagei Shav V'HaEmet*, I enumerated many of the false concepts which people believe to be correct though they are bound

36

by the chains of vanity....Truly, the struggle against vain moral concepts should be based on reason and morality, and not by twisting *halakhah* for our own purposes. It would be a disservice to turn the holy *mitzvot* into irrelevant teachings that would be as double-edged swords in the hands of scholars with little understanding...with which to destroy that which is good and beneficial in our hopes to rebuild our nation. We must consider everything both from the standpoint of morality and of reason, that which we consider proper, honest and correct and able to stand on the two foundations [of morality and reason]. Then we must look at *halakhah* whose "ways are pleasant, whose paths are peace" and which certainly contains nothing contrary to reason, and what stands to reason and morality. And if [on the surface] we see something which does seem contrary, we must grapple with it until we find that it is not devoid of these elements, otherwise we have not understood either *halakhah* or morality. But to reject everything that is good and beneficial in our people using the principle of *halakhic* rigorousity is not what was intended by the saying: "blessed be those who are rigorous" (*ibid.*, Part 4, p. 10).

The rulings of the early adjudicators are, of course, binding, but we must probe deeply into their reasoning and their moral and religious intentions to understand how to apply them to present-day life.

The second assumption is linked to the first, but adds a dimension of distinctly modern refinement and, it should be emphasized, Hirschensohn was well aware of its modernity. In our time, to probe *halakhah*, one must add the dimension of historical research in its broadest sense for without an understanding of the historical reality behind *halakhah* one cannot delve into the "soul of Scripture." This position clearly emanates from a knowledge of the swift historical changes which the Jewish people have undergone in recent generations. If, in the light of an early source, we want to know what the *halakhic* ruling is for our day, we must be aware of what the historical reality was of the adjudicators in order to reach the correct conclusions for today's different historical reality. This is a principle that Hirschensohn often used. At one point, in explaining the difference between his and Maimonides' stance, he wrote that Maimonides was not sensitive to historical understanding in its modern sense, and that he was not deterred by obvious anachronisms. A knowledge of history influences the understanding of *halakhah* and must influence a *halakhic* ruling as well.

It should be emphasized that taking the historical dimension into consideration does not mean regarding *halakhah* relativistically — despite the fact that Hirschensohn was well aware of history's cultural progress. He did not, however, view progress as an absolute gauge for interpreting the Torah on the highest principle plane, as is clearly implied in his polemic with Rabbi Kook. Hirschensohn, too, believed that we learn true morality from Torah, but his perception was that we must delve into it to the best of our spiritual ability which is an outgrowth of our own times. Using this approach, it would appear that the underlying meaning of Hirschensohn's somewhat obscure sentence in his letter to Rabbi Reuven Margoliot can be understood.

> True, the difference between us is that you progress from the historical to the *halakhah*, which is to say that you view *halakhah* in a historical perspective. Whereas I learn about history from *halakhah*; that is, I weigh history from a *halakhic* standpoint. But the onlooker might think the difference between us is the opposite because you write history and I write *halakhah* (*ibid.*, p. 196).

Hirschensohn should perhaps be understood as follows. Writing *halakhah* while taking into consideration the historical reality of every stage of its formation can give the impression that the author is dealing only with an historical interpretation of *halakhah*. His intention, however, was to base himself on the eternal ethical and religious principles of *halakhah*, applying them to the changing historical reality; only by so doing would it be possible to go from the *halakhic*-historical to the *halakhic* ruling now binding in the contemporary setting. In this way, not only is the *halakhic* principle understood in depth, but so is the manner in which the principle has been applied in given historical realities. Thus, the historic nature of a *halakhic* ruling becomes evident and, from the way in which the ruling was decreed, the historical situation is revealed. In any event, it is clear that Hirschensohn believed that change in the application of *halakhah* does not imply any relativity in regard to its principles. These are eternal and binding at any time.

The third assumption deals with the authority of contemporary rabbinical scholars. From the beginning Hirschensohn was very much against the manner in which the saying, "the early [adjudicators] were like angels" was understood by the scholars of his day. The adage, he argued, should be said by the greatest scholars of a generation because of the humility it demonstrates toward the scholars of earlier generations. But when ordinary people and students repeat it, it is no longer a matter of humility but of hampering the authority of the generation's great adjudicators to determine *halakhah* for their day.

Those who hold that the great adjudicators of each generation do not have the authority to make *halakhic* rulings based on their best understanding and according to the reality of their time, Hirschensohn believed, trample Israel's glory to the ground. Nor did he stop there but accused them of being "heretics who observe religion" for in their overzealousness they strike at the essential root of the Oral Law (*ibid.*, end of Part 1). Hirschensohn was referring not only to the self-awareness of rabbis and the attitude of the people toward them, but also to a principle that he applied. The authority of scholars is not anchored exclusively or even chiefly in the authority of the teachers who agree with them, it is anchored in the Jewish public. The scholars' responsibility to their people is obligatory, and that responsibility is placed on them by the Torah. If there is a Jewish public that needs *halakhic* guidance in questions which derive from a historical reality, the scholars of the generation are required to respond to such needs. This obligation toward the people which is cast upon them by the Torah is actually the source of the scholars' authority even if it means differing from rulings made in the past by the greatest scholars. Thus, the authority of the adjudicators has by no means lessened as their charge toward the people who wish to receive religious guidance is the source of that authority (see *Malki BaKodesh*, Part 2, Questions A and B).

In summary, these three assumptions together comprise the theoretical foundation for Haim Hirschensohn's unusual *halakhic* audaciousness; they serve to guide him in his detailed discussions of every issue.

The assumptions facilitate a broad-scoped *halakhic* approach, just how far-reaching can be seen by examining a major problem that affects life in a modern Jewish state: "the matter of decrees with which the body politic cannot live." The way in which Hirschensohn formulated the question is sufficient indication of his daring, and the elaboration is consistent and forceful.

The conditions of life for a people in Exile, whether wandering from province to province and region to region, or having found peace as a sojourner in a land grateful to its sovereigns for receiving them for better or worse, are different from those of a people who live in freedom in their own land according to their own norms, character, concepts, aspirations and desires, and all else they consider important. The decrees and qualified restrictions which the scholars were commanded to proclaim in order to guard and protect the Torah were always made with wisdom and knowledge and a broad view that took into account the people's actual situation (see Tractate Shabbat, 113:b). Many of the rulings were made in accordance with the living conditions in a particular diaspora; these would be neither adequate nor beneficial for the moment when we achieve our freedom and wish for Israel to be like all other nations.

While we were living the life of Exile the limitations on us could be likened to telling a Nazirite (who has sworn to abstain) not to go near the vineyard. After all, the Nazirite's soul has long since recoiled from the fruit of the vine...for he vowed to abstain. We need not burn down the vineyard and turn it into a wasteland so that there is no vineyard near the Nazirite to tempt him to evil; it is enough to warn him to go around and not approach it. So the fences (around the Torah) have been enough to preserve Jewish ethics. For the life of Exile suppressed our spirit and caused our souls to loathe every exaggerated pleasure and vile passion, and setting up fences was sufficient to prevent our stumbling should we have followed our hearts and eyes. Similarly, in the time of the Second Temple when the rulers of Persia and Medes, the Greeks and the Romans, were in the Land of Israel and could not be opposed.

This is not the case for a free people whose nature is the desire to luxuriate in everything good. For an independent people, the spirit is not dimmed and fences which negate its freedom are of no use to it whatsoever. On the contrary, restrictions will cause the people to rebel and they will insist on their right to the freedom which is in their soul, for the spirit cannot be bound. In order to guard morality in conditions of freedom, obstacles must be completely removed — do not encumber the soul with restrictions but limit the stumbling blocks so that they do not encroach on its borders. This will be done not by fettering the soul, but by providing it with moral joys to awaken it so that it can revel in wisdom and knowledge, aspire to ideals which give great pleasure, and illuminate the eyes of the people so that they themselves choose the moral and good and abhor the immoral, just as the soul loathes everything putrid and rotten like tables laden with dung.

This will be the task of the great leaders of Israel, its wise men, rabbis and judges. Whether the ordination [of sages] is renewed or not, there will be one primary task for the Sanhedrin: to infuse the living people with a spiritual life. This task will certainly be given to them for it will be their obligation as the shepherds "who will tend you with knowledge and skill" (Jeremiah 3:15). Whether their authority is known as ordination or by some other name makes no difference; they must strive through knowledge and wisdom to strengthen both the nationhood and religion of Israel so that life does not hamper religion and religion does not hamper life. The guardianship established by the wise men of Israel will not be as a guard over us to ensure that we do not deviate from the path of morality, but as a safeguard to make sure that immorality does not enter our boundaries. And just as the *mitzvah* of "You shall keep My charge" (Leviticus 18:30) is incumbent upon the wise men of Israel to build fences when the conditions of life require it, so will it be incumbent upon them when the conditions of life demand "the discharge of their duties" (Numbers 8:26) to use their power to permit that which is preferable to stringencies which will not repair religion and life.

It will also be one of the steps of Elijah and his Bet Din to cancel all contingent decrees, except for those eighteen noted in Tractate Avodah Zarah, 36:1. They will have to cancel those customs which have no basis in *halakhah* — the norms that were adopted from the Gentiles by Jews who learned gentile ways while mingling with them, norms which the ignorant thought to be Torah. They will also have to cancel those decrees which derive from conditions no longer relevant but whose cancellation requires another Bet Din, and to invalidate those rulings which are self-nullifying — even as far as the law is concerned

— and do not even require a Bet Din to cancel them. Really, they must make the effort so that a religion of rote does not block the development of a new life and nationhood in the Land of Israel where we will be sovereign, the Lord God over us, and shake off the mire with which the Galut burdened us: the customs of different countries which caused religion and *halakhah* to be neglected because of the views of ignorant plutocrats, unlettered ignorants and women who bowed to astrology.

But the reforms of the people must be based on religion and *halakhah*, not on Reformers who think that reform means breaking through the wall of religion when all they need to do is to open the door in accordance with Torah and *halakhah*; all the while the Lord will be with us and will be our fortress, and the Land will be ours, governed by a Jewish political leadership.

There are issues which could arise in the life of the state which could appear to be incompatible with immutable *halakhic* rulings that were issued by the rabbis when Israel was in Exile or when there was a foreign domination over the Land, for it was only under those circumstances that the majority of Jews could maintain such laws, in a time before there was significant progress in the world in general, or in Israel in particular. We must now use *halakhah* precisely to terminate those laws.

In the first instance we must see if there is a way to cancel that which was forbidden by the rabbis in accordance with the ruling that a decree which has not spread to most of Israel can be canceled by a minor Bet Din. This is based on the words of the Rashbag (Rabbi Simeon ben Gamaliel) and Rabbi Eliezer Bar Zaddok who said: the public should not be burdened with a decree unless most can carry it out; it is better to cancel those decrees which can be canceled rather than let the people take it upon themselves to do so. For even of those matters forbidden by the Torah, it is said: leave Israel alone for it is better that they err than willfully transgress the law (Tractate Betzah, p. 30).

There is no doubt that because of this Rabbi Samlai said about Rabbi Yehudah Hanassi that if he permitted the use of the idolators' oil in his historic situation, will you not permit the use of their bread in our day? (Avodah Zarah, 37:1). Which is to say that if in our day the people have doubts and [the issue is so dimmed for them] they have acted in an unrestrained way, it would be better to permit the bread just as once the oil was permitted. For if we let every matter with which the polity cannot live simply fall into disuse, it will harm the spiritual life of our people. If this is done there will be more holes in the fence than there is a whole fence; the barricade of our religion will be in such bad repair, God forbid, that it will not be able to stand and there will be nothing that can be done about it.

Thus the wise men, who are progressive rather than reactionary in examining contemporary needs, should precede the breakdown of authority by providing safety valves lest the people, themselves, break through and transgress those boundaries set by the early adjudicators; the leaders shall not be transgressors: "Men from your midst shall rebuild ancient ruins, You shall restore foundations laid long ago. And you shall be called 'Repairer of fallen walls, Restorer of lanes for habitation'" (Isaiah 58:12) — (*Malki BaKodesh*, Part 2, pp. 7-8).

The excerpt illustrates how Hirschensohn used the three assumptions noted above. From the manner in which he presented the issue, it is not surprising that he was prepared to go as far as he did in proposals that were a departure from the *halakhah* as set down for generations. Nonetheless, as he notes, his outlook is not that of the Reform. For even if *halakhic* restrictions are to be canceled, it must be done by means of *halakhah*; in other words, by using the rules set down by *halakhah* for those areas. This distinction is solidly rooted in Hirschensohn's assumptions. Based on common sense, reasoning is attuned and tied to *halakhah*. It is anchored in the principles which were adduced from the *halakhic* details of the way in which the ruling was made, and it reconstructs the sense in which *halakhah* was interpreted in its time in order to apply that reasoning to the conditions of our day. But Hirschensohn's regard for the historical dimension goes only so far. To be precise, he does not interpret the progress he finds in contemporary culture as a development capable of turning the Torah itself into a historical work relative to its time. The Torah is from God and eternally valid; it relates to history from a plane which is beyond any historical development.

What can be learned by looking at *halakhah* from a historical viewpoint is its relationship to history — not just in general, but in specific issues as well. Here the framework of the discussion must be widened in order to clarify an important basic assumption.

There are, indeed, in Hirschensohn's writings, evaluations of a general nature on the dissimilarities between different historical periods, such as the contrast between life in Exile under foreign rulers and life in an independent state. However, this general evaluation can never provide sufficient reason for changing *halakhah*. Change can be based only on a detailed knowledge of conditions and an understanding of the complex difficulties that are liable to cause a rift between a *halakhic* ruling and the way the people live. Only when the *halakhic* adjudicator knows, or can surmise with great certainty and in detail, what the burden of observance would be for the observant Jew, can he find a solution. He would then be able "to think clearly and logically about what must be done according to the Torah that would not interfere with life, and how to use life so as not to fail in the observance of Torah" (*ibid.*, p. 108). Not only is this so because of the importance of considering the public's ability to live with a situation and what is vital to its existence and welfare, but primarily because study for the sake of a viable *halakhic* ruling in actual circumstances, illuminates *halakhah* and reveals its meanings. It is precisely against a background of reality that *halakhah* can be more profoundly understood and its implications for the new reality drawn upon. Thus, Hirschensohn's interpretation of the *halakhah* which deals with entering the Temple Mount is different from that of Maimonides.

> The real reason for this is that the early adjudicators did not deal with issues as a practical matter, but only as a remote possibility. As he is immersed in study, every scholar and rabbi knows to what extent he can engage in conjecture and raise *halakhic* possibilities about questions which are not actual...and in the seven hundred years from Maimonides until the present time, entering the Temple Mount was not a practical issue....This is no longer the case, and now that we are actually confronted by this weighty issue we can see that the ban could raise serious problems for Israel (*ibid.*, pp. 110-115).

Here is an indication of the profundity of Hirschensohn's conclusions about history which he drew from *halakhah* because it was a knowledge of historical detail that illuminated the depth of *halakhah* for him. In any event, his approach is completely at variance with that of the Reform who regard historic reality as though it is

44

inherently possessed of ethical and religious criteria that are unilaterally binding on *halakhah*.

Finally, for Hirschensohn the authority of the wise men of each generation to renew *halakhic* rulings is not bound by these historically-conditioned moral and religious criteria. Moreover, it is not the personal stature of the adjudicators that is important, but their obligation toward the people based on the Torah. Therefore, the Torah requires a thorough study of *halakhah* as the adjudicators understand its place in the circumstances of the life of the people, at a given time.

> Even when referring to the cancellation of "a number of rulings set down in rabbinic decrees..." it is precisely on the basis of *halakhah* that we must consider how to cancel them (*ibid.*).

On the basis of these assumptions Hirschensohn reasoned that when difficulties arise between life and the Torah, difficulties that can be factually and precisely — not just theoretically or generally — defined, and for which norms have not yet been set, either by those who adhere to a strict interpretation of existing *halakhah*, or by those who rebel against *halakhah*, when matters get so out of hand, it is time for wise *halakhists* to act, because, afterwards, "sophistry will not help." "For the winds will rage," Hirschensohn contends, "and the storm will not subside before it wreaks its damage in all four corners of the house and entraps the young" (*ibid.*, p. 108). But if matters have not reached such an extreme point, it is possible to find a positive solution by probing deeply into the details of the relevant *halakhic* rulings. The scholar who objectively understands the difficulties involved, and who is prepared to fathom the "soul" of *halakhah* — its intent at the time of the ruling — will be capable of solving every problem. Hirschensohn's *halakhic* undertaking was typified by this approach in many sectors of his work.

Chapter 6

ON A DEMOCRATIC STATE ACCORDING TO HALAKHAH

Haim Hirschensohn, as has been shown, perceived of national-ism as essentially democratic, as an expression of the equality and autonomy of individuals participating in the life of a greater whole. In discussing the relationship between Torah and life, Hirschensohn reflects on and interprets his notion that nationalism is a framework for the self-expression of a people and its independence.

For Rabbi Hirschensohn, the authority of the Sages is grounded in the Torah which holds them responsible to the people. The extent to which the needs of the people and its desires are seen as having an influence on the way *halakhah* was determined will be seen below. But, even at this stage, it is clear that there is a tension between a democracy rooted in Jewish tradition and a modern political democracy as it is practiced in the free countries of the West (from which Hirschensohn undoubtedly drew much inspiration). A close examination of the Western democratic ideal shows that the substantive difference stems from the perception of Torah as having a supra-human authority. It would appear that this is the root of both manifest and latent ambiguity in Hirschensohn's writings.

What influence did the modern democratic ideal have on Hirschensohn's thought? He became acquainted with the idea as embodied in American political and social life; indeed, the demo-cratic pathos characteristic of American society permeates his writ-ings. This pathos seems to have inspired his positive view of modern Western culture so that he became open and liberal not only vis-a-vis individuals and streams within Jewry, but toward all human beings. In other words, Hirschensohn discovered the great affinity between American democracy and the spirit of biblical prophecy and responded to it with unequivocal enthusiasm. If the meaning of democracy is self-government by the people where the common will is the source of legislative authority and the common good is the purpose of government, if the meaning of democracy is individual liberty, freedom of thought and absolute equality before the law regardless of religious or ethnic origin, social class, educational

47

background or sex, and if the meaning of democracy is a far-reaching mutual tolerance, a liberal attitude toward other people's opinions and customs, love of mankind and an openness to intellectual pluralism, all within the unifying framework of morality and respect for the law, and finally, if the meaning of democracy is attention to the importance of individual and social success by cultivating the natural human aspiration toward the improvement of one's material and spiritual conditions so that human creativity is enhanced and happiness achieved, then Haim Hirschensohn may be described as a fervent and consistent democrat.

Hirschensohn was convinced that, as described above, democracy was in complete accord with Torah; on the conceptual plane, this was simple and apparent. The purpose of national government in a democracy (as noted at the conclusion of the preceding paragraph) is particularly relevant to Hirschensohn's repeated emphasis on the practical and "this-worldly" nature of Judaism, guiding man toward material and spiritual well-being in *this* life. Thus, in Hirschensohn's treatise, *Musagei Shav V'HaEmet*, which was significantly influenced by American positivism, the closing article is entitled, "The Aspect of Life in Jewish Religion and Religious Philosophy." It is characteristic of his entire approach. The article claims that even Jewish theology is not exclusively interested in metaphysical concerns, but expresses rather a will to understand reality in order to uncover and verify the assumptions necessary to confront that reality. This attitude permeates all of Hirschensohn's writings. It is informed by a desire to affect contemporary life and to address the practical issues of the day. At the end of Section One of *Malki BaKodesh*, Hirschensohn writes that even his purely intellectual undertakings were intended only to deal with the pressing issues of the day which is what the rabbis had always done. Indeed, it was to the extent that they responded meaningfully to real life dilemmas that their spiritual endeavors stood the test of time.

This orientation of philosophy to life is the essence of the democratic tradition, and Hirschensohn was entirely aware of it. He points to it specifically in the introduction to *Malki BaKodesh* when he defines the difference between his essay and the responsa literature of sages in previous generations.

My book is not the result of particular incidents, but rather of general events which were the outcome of various stages in our people's development. The questions were not posed by individuals alone, but by the entire nation, and their answers are directed to the nation as a whole (*op. cit.*, Part One, p. 20).

The quotation can be summarized by paraphrasing a well-known democratic aphorism: these are questions from the people, about the people, and answered for the people. It was of utmost importance that the entire people learn and know the *halakhic* rulings which regulated their lives, not only so that they might express an opinion but to help determine standards of appropriate behavior. In this way, obedience to the Law becomes conscious and voluntary since it is born of true understanding.

To Rabbi Hirschensohn's mind, the essence of the relationship between religion and nationalism in Judaism is the Torah as the covenant made with the people of Israel. For him, this momentous occasion laid the foundation for a pure democracy that maintains national independence since the covenantal status of society articulates the voluntary commitment of the members of the nation to each other and, together, to God. Hirschensohn frequently reiterated his view of the covenant as the basis of the Torah's hegemony over the people. For example:

In my humble opinion, this is the underpinning for one of the great principles of Jewish faith — of its religion and nationality; it is the pillar of the entire Torah and the commandments. It is one of the basics of our faith that the Holy One, Blessed be He, did not set Himself up as a tyrant over His creatures, and just as He does not want one man to rule over another except for his good, so He would not want to force anyone to observe the commandments against his will nor to enter the Covenant at Sinai and desert of Moab unless these commandments were accepted willingly....God does not wish to appear as an overlord toward the people of Israel but to be their Lord by entering into a covenantal relationship with them....Whatever the case, it is clear to us that the people of Israel took a voluntary oath to live according to the Torah and its commandments, and inherent in that vow is the true national bond in which the individual renounces his self-interest in favor of the group, and each person commits himself to the greater whole....The result of this is that our obligation to the Torah and to every one of the Divine commandments is grounded in this covenant and is not by virtue of the authority of the nation's wise men, judges and elders. For if the Torah had been forced on the people, then it would have been a decree from above rather than a voluntary act of acceptance of the Law, in accordance with God's will. Only after the nation was united by entering into the covenant and willingly promised to observe the Law did the people choose judges and elders from among themselves to ensure the guardianship of their oath, as is the case whenever any nation accepts a constitution *ab initio*, only afterwards delegating authority to judges and officials of the people. This was the rule not only at Sinai, but everywhere and at all times in Jewish history....

So we see that the Courts are invested with power by public consent, and without this the Courts are powerless....Yet if we are talking about the power of the entire nation, we must note that, as seen in Tractate Horayot, 3:2, the rabbis said: since the majority agrees, the individual or the minority must accept the decision of the majority. This is stated explicitly in the Torah *(Malki BaKodesh*, Part 3, pp. 80-81).

Hirschensohn's *Eileh Divrei HaBrit* is a three-part *halakhic-* historical analysis of all of the covenants noted in the Bible. His aim in this work is a systematic and developmental exposition of the concept of the covenant in Judaism, based on the assumption that both the political and religious aspects of Jewish nationalism evolved from a series of covenants. Each covenant defined a specific facet of national life according to the needs of the time: the relationship between the Patriarchs and God; between the people and God; between individual members of the nation and between the tribes; the covenant determining settlement of the Land of Israel, and the covenants between Israel and other nations. For Hirschensohn, the covenant is the basis of all authentic human relationships.

What then is the essential quality of the covenant? A passage parallel to the one quoted above stresses the uniqueness of the biblical covenant even more conclusively than the previous segment.

And the most wondrous result of all this is that the obligation to observe the commandments, according to the opinion of all the Talmudists, was not an order since the Holy One, Blessed be He, did not set Himself up as a tyrant over his creatures but desired rather that they accept His will voluntarily. We took God's plan as expressed in His Torah and made it into our covenant, accepting also our sages' innovations which ultimately earned the status of law.

It is in this sense that Judaism is superior to all other religions that only have commandments which they believe in as having been decreed. Though our religion contains a great many commandments whose origins are in God's supreme plan, nonetheless, we have committed ourselves to observing them not by virtue of decree, but out of free will, just as any constitution is upheld by a nation when it is in harmony with the will of the people. Therefore, ours is a national religion, and theirs is a religion of faith. In this way, other people have "religion," whereas the Jews have the Torah, just laws and statues which they took upon themselves in response to God's plan....

And even as the character of the laws are different...so is the nature of punishment. In other nations, one who disobeys the law may not defend himself by claiming forgetfulness or ignorance of the law: the law is to be obeyed as an order, and the transgressor is punished for not having bothered to become familiar with it....This is not the case in Judaism where law and punishment stem from the same basis, for punishment is the outcome of sin since the transgressor transgressed a voluntary commitment to the law. Furthermore, by accepting the entire system of Torah upon himself, the Jew accepts as well the responsibility of knowing every detail of the law since the whole is the sum of its parts (*Beirurei HaMidot*, Part 1, pp. 288-89).

The crucial point is that the covenant is a voluntary and binding commitment. There can be neither an element of coercion nor a preceding decree to be obeyed. Both sides to the agreement recognize their common interest and declare their mutual obligation before the law. A symbolic act serves as a testimony to the covenant for all future generations, making the agreement legally binding, so that its conditions subsequently become compulsory.

The singularity of the Jewish people is expressed firstly in the fact that their organization as a nation is based on a covenant. Two qualifications must be added. Hirschensohn believed that every nation is organized along legal lines, meaning that nationhood is based necessarily upon the mutual obligation of its members to each other and toward the group as a whole. What distinguishes the Jewish people from all others is that the Jews were the first group in history to frame a nationality devoid of a preceding coercion. The Jews agreed among themselves to become a nation and set their decision by means of the covenant. Secondly, Hirschensohn stressed the distinction between what he called the "Divine covenant" and the "national covenant." By "Divine covenant," he meant the agreement between certain individuals (the Patriarchs) and God, or between the people and God. At the core of both covenants is the acknowledgment of God's hegemony, on the one hand, and the observance that is required of individuals and the people, on the other.

The "national covenant" is the commitment that each member of the nation makes to the specific code of behavior as a people.[1] Though integrally related, the two types of covenant are not interchangeable in the sense that only a national covenant can ratify a covenant between a people and its God. Nationalism, according to Hirschensohn, therefore precedes and determines religion in Judaism. The Jews as the Chosen People face their God, although, as such, nationality is a preparation for religious singularity. God's plan for the nation to observe His law precedes the people's commitment to nationhood in accordance with Divine authority.

The interdependence of the "national covenant" and the "Divine covenant" is unique to Judaism, adding a dimension to Jewish nationality which differentiates it absolutely from all other nationalities.

> It seems to me that the contract in Judaism as expressed uniquely in the Divine covenant is more than a political concept. All of the ramifications of the contract as it is understood in Judaism are implicit in the phrase "a blessing or a curse of the community" and "a blessing or a curse of the individual." The community blessing or curse should be understood within the national-political context as a reference to the moral-legal imperative inherent in the constitution of a given state. Accursed is "he who does not observe all of the Torah." The constitutional framework simply means that all citizens are responsible to each other to uphold the constitution, not in terms of an interpersonal obligation, but as an expression of personal loyalty to the state and its laws.

The same is true in the religious sphere in that no person can observe even one small detail of a commandment for another person since the law is not personal, nor is it the obligation of the individual alone, rather it is communal. As the law is universally obligatory, no person can observe it for another; each individual must perform his duty himself. But what is meant by the passage, "Blessed is he as an individual; cursed is he as an individual concerning the details of each and every commandment," according to Rashi, is a different obligation. The liability here is a personal one, as we learn from the words "and they shall stumble one because of another" which means because of another's transgression. This is more than a political duty. Every man becomes responsible for his fellow-man, just as members of a family are responsible for one another. This is not only a political concept but a religious one as expressed by our religion's commandments of reproof: "And thou shalt reprove thy brother." Now, if a political dimension is added to the religious obligation of the individual to uphold the religious-social contract, the result is a similar type of state. This is especially true of Judaism as its national life is the soul of the laws and the Torah. We therefore must make a distinction between the "covenants of nations" and the "Jewish national covenant." A "national covenant" is a universally-binding contract, as we have shown. Every person is responsible for maintaining the laws of the state. Just as the social contract is binding on the totality, similarly it is not only on the totality nor only on an individual but on the state as a whole and on every individual only as a partner to the contract by virtue of his being a member of society.

Of course, a people is comprised of a larger number of individuals, more than there are in a family or tribe. Therefore, they have no individual responsibility towards each other. But the Jewish national covenant is a special case. Granted that a national covenant is merely a collective bonding, nonetheless in this general bonding there is a special interrelationship of individuals for a mutual responsibility in which each is responsible individually for his brother and his brother's undertaking to uphold the community, for this is not an individual matter.

Here lies the difference from the American concept alluded to above in which a person who does not decry wrongdoing is simply called a "bad citizen," but a witness to evil who keeps silent in time of war is subject to the death penalty since his silence jeopardizes the welfare of the state. The Jew, who is constantly defending his religion, is always in a holy war. Thus, he who has the opportunity to protest when necessary and declines to do so is guilty of a capital offense. Moreover, since all other Jews are responsible for him, he is called a transgressor against each individual Jew. The Jewish religion has defined the appropriate punishment for all those who have an opportunity to speak out against evil and refrain from doing so (*Eileh Divrei HaBrit*, Part 2, pp. 63-64).

In other words, the commitment to God is a personal commitment made by each individual. As a result, every person is responsible before God not only to society as a whole but, to the extent that his deed impacts on society, to every member of society. This is also true for relations between different sectors of the nation, or between tribes.

In the same way, the tribes have a special obligation to each other since Israel is one nation, despite the fact that it is divided into twelve tribes. We have some indication of this in the United States of America. The American constitution attempted to model the nation on the Bible. Consequently, the country was divided into separate states...and though each state has its own special statutes, all the states — with a star representing each one — are united under one flag; each must be loyal to the federal union which unites all of them in mutual responsibility. Now, for the Jewish state there is an added dimension to this mutual responsibility. What holds for relationships between individuals, as I have explained, holds for the tribes....Israelite tribal unity differs qualitatively from state unity in America since the latter is manifested only in matters pertinent to the United States as a whole, and the federal government is not allowed to intervene in the internal matters of any state. This is not the case among the tribes of Israel. Though their separateness is expressed by their flags, in matters of injustice or infringements of morality, or ritual concerns, each of the tribes is responsible for the other (*op. cit.*, Part 3, p. 33).

Comparing the two passages quoted above with the initial assumption that the essence of the covenant is in its acceptance out of free will results in a paradox. A social order of far-reaching commitment was shaped on a foundation of personal liberty, free of any preceding pressure or constraint. This was unique on two scores: the covenantal society of the Israelites was characterized by its voluntary underpinning which went so far as to insist on the consent by each and every individual to the conditions of the covenant; at the same time, a commitment was demanded of the community and from each individual — as an affiliate of the community — to maintain the covenant. In both instances, the link between the "covenant of the people" and "the Divine covenant" is expressed in the special religious topology of national rule. This factor bears emphasis because it is a condition for understanding a number of Hirschensohn's practical conclusions.

Hirschensohn attributed the unique religious character in the social relationships of the Jews to the difference in behavior prescribed vis-a-vis a fellow Jew on certain matters and that which is prescribed vis-a-vis a Gentile. He also attributed the difference between the status of men and women in certain matters to the unique religious character of Torah legislation. It is in this uniqueness that the relative incompatibility of the democratic ideals of the Torah to the secular democratic notion can be seen.

But even before we come to these issues, a question must be asked. How does the consistent, direct, voluntary dimension of each individual become compatible with the absolute obligation of the individual? More particularly, how can a covenant entered into by a specific generation continue to obligate those who were not present when the covenant was made? If truth be told, Hirschensohn was not overly concerned by the first part of the question. His assumption was that once a person undertook, before God and his people, to enter the covenant, it obliged him totally and any retreat from his obligation justified the use of pressure as prescribed in the law. Furthermore, once the individual consented to the conditions of the covenant, he was obliged to obey the decisions of those in whom the covenant had vested power, in light of their understanding, both to interpret the laws and to take on additional obligations in the name of the community.

When serving as the emissaries of the people, or even of a particular section of the public, the delegates become "heads," that is, leaders, of the people in the matter for which they were deputized...therefore, just as the covenant of the forefathers applies to the descendants, in the same way the covenant of the leaders applies to them. Just as the leaders can disclaim public ownership, expropriate or protest and curse, etc., so they can administer oaths...and the power to administer oaths applies also to take oaths on behalf of the community, and to take oaths from others on their behalf and to make a covenant, and the covenant will be binding on the entire people, even on those not yet born, for no covenant is made at a meeting of the entire people, but it is made rather by the heads for the people. The only condition is that the leaders must be chosen and appointed in accordance with the laws of the particular people, after which they become delegates and emissaries of that people; in this context each delegate and emissary of the people, by the powers vested in him, becomes a head of the people — but his selection must be according to the laws of that particular people concerning the election of representatives (*ibid.*, p. 43).

The second part of the question preoccupied Rabbi Hirschensohn, presumably because of its topicality. What is the basis for obliging our generation to accept commitments taken by our ancestors in all the covenant-setting occasions of ancient times? The answer which Hirschensohn offered is based on a general proposition which relates to the constitution of a people, and on a particular proposition which relates to the constitution of the people of Israel.

The laws of any people apply equally to those who have not yet been born [Hirschensohn claimed], since no people can be expected to renew its laws in every generation. This is a simple and easily understood concept. Therefore, when Israel became a people, there was no need for the covenant to be interpreted to those as yet unborn, also a clear and understandable point. In order to make the covenant binding on the entire people, however, God had to make it apply equally to those yet to be born (*op. cit.*, Part 1, p. 76).

The general assumption, therefore, is that since a covenant of the people already exists, its validity applies to all legislation made within its framework. As long as the people exists, the national legislation ensuing from the covenant applies to the generations which follow. (We would not seem to be deviating from Rabbi Hirschensohn's understanding if we added the proviso that this legislation applies as long as the institutions empowered under the conditions of the covenant have not legislated to the contrary.) The initial covenant, however, must be specifically phrased in a way which makes it apply to subsequent generations. In the above passage, Rabbi Hirschensohn does not justify the legal basis underlying the possibility of applying the covenant in this manner. Does this not contradict his principle that each person must relate personally and directly to the covenant? The answer to this point is found at another point in the same book.

It is indeed true that a covenant can set down rules which apply as well to the generations that follow, as I have explained at length...but this is only with respect to those who will be born later. That which was meted out for the fathers subsumes everything that is considered part of them, including children yet to be born, their potential and vitality...as I paraphrased in the name of Rabbi Behai, of blessed memory, the father is the root of the sons, and the sons are the branches meant to come forth from the root, and therefore it is within the potential of this root to bring forth the generations to follow. Small children already born, however, have ceased to be dependent on the root and any covenant which the adults accept applies only to the adults themselves; branches which have already stemmed from the root are not included. Through the *mitzvah* to educate which obliges a man to instruct his sons when they are small in all those things that he feels religion and morality require so that the children will not deviate from these things when they are adults or even in their old age, the father can use his power over his sons to bind them to the covenant, and this shall be binding on them as adults, for the covenant is not only an oath but also a decree and a consecration, but the children must be mentioned specifically in the covenant so that it carries the force of a rule which will apply to them when they become adults (*op. cit.*, Part 3, p. 119).

At first glance this quote seems extremely strange; indeed, it would appear to contradict the basic principle of the covenant, namely that each individual must accept it for himself. It is, therefore, of the utmost importance to understand its precise meaning. Does it imply that any commitment made by parents applies to their children? Can parents oblige their children to accept anything which seems important to them? The answer to both questions is without doubt negative. In a passage close to the passage quoted above from the first part of *Eileh Divrei HaBrit,* Rabbi Hirschensohn states categorically:

> A covenant or an oath or a consecration taken on by someone in his individual capacity does not apply to his children. We have never heard of an oath or vow of a private individual obliging his sons, as detailed in *Yoreh Deah* (4, 228, para. 35), even if a man commits himself to something by an oath and handshake, and subsequently dies, his inheritors are not bound by his oath...and thus the sons are not bound by the Covenant of Abraham, for at that point they were still not a "people," and the Holy One, Blessed be He, had to make a specific covenant with the sons of Abraham (which is why it is written "between" your seed which follows you) so that although a father cannot oblige his son to accept a covenant or oath, even if he specifically mentions his intention to do so, the covenant here is not with the father on behalf of the sons but rather with the sons themselves (*op. cit.,* Part 1, p. 74).

In other words, Rabbi Hirschensohn adheres to the basic principle of the covenant that each individual must accept it for himself. This principle applies to offspring as well. How, then, can this position be reconciled with the assertion that children are an ontological continuation of their parents, with the duty of education placed on the parents? The solution lies in the short but definitive sentence which closes the earlier passage "...the covenant is not only an oath but also a decree and a consecration," and the potential of the people, "but the children must be mentioned specifically in the covenant." The key phrase is "the potential of the people," referring both to the regenerative power of the parents as the basis for the ongoing existence of the people, and to the duty of education which implements the authority of the people since by definition a "people" refers to an ongoing continuity across the generations.

As an individual, no person has the right to impose on others a commitment which he has taken on himself — neither as a progenitor nor as an educator. Children are not to be seen as an ontological continuation of their parents' individual existence. As an individual, each person is a world in his own right. On the other hand, from the outset, the people, or nation, represents a unity of generations, and it is to be defined in its generations just as the individual is defined through the years of his life. In the same way that an individual can make commitments in the present concerning the future, so the people can commit itself in the present concerning the future since, from the point of view of the people — the ontology of the generations — the children yet unborn are already part of the overall being of the people, and they are present in potential form through those who are present in tangible form. Those not yet born are, therefore, bound by all the commitments which stem from the constituting covenant. The implication of this, however, is that this obligation (to respect existing commitments) stems not from the parents as individuals, but from the parents as representatives of the people, both in their essence as progenitors and in their actions as educators. The "potential of the people" supports them as they bring their children after them into the "covenant of the people."

These comments relate to a general assumption concerning all peoples. A specific assumption rests in the unique nature of the covenant between Israel and its God. It could be said that at the moment of this covenant all the generations were actually present and accepted the constitution of the people.

It is true that we do not deal with the arcane and all spiritualism is concealed and known to the Lord our God alone. Yet it is obvious that things which no individual can do and which cannot happen in a purely human context can and do occur in conjunction with the Holy One, Blessed be He, who remembers the act of creating the world and commands all the creatures of His creation in antiquity, in a way which is understood by the sage in accordance with his faith, by the philosopher in accordance with his philosophy and by the mystic in accordance with his musings. All these are building blocks for the *halakhist* in his work who sees that the Holy One, Blessed be He, can make a covenant with those of his creatures whom we, in reality, do not yet consider part of the world, but who exist in a potential form through their links with the souls of those who exist today....And whereas we, who are the roots, cannot contact those whom our soul will send forth as branches, the Holy One, Blessed be He, can touch them (*op. cit.*, p. 78).

Of course, here, too, one observes the qualitative difference between the people of Israel and other peoples, a difference whose thrust is the validity and eternity of the covenant.

This is the difference between Israel and the other peoples. Other peoples, who have evolved through their consanguinity and in their own lands, are natural peoples devoid of a covenant because their blood and their land are their bond; this is why they are called "peoples of the earth" for it is through their ties to their land that they developed into peoples. Their laws apply to yet unborn as the lore of that people. If such a people is exiled from its own land and their blood intermingled, they lose their character as a people....This is not the case with the people of Israel who became a people not by virtue of their land, for they were living in an alien land. Nor does the intermingling of their blood alter their nationality, for even the souls that Abraham won over in Horan became converts, and when the Israelites left Egypt many other peoples came with them. Throughout the Oral Law we have examples such as Rabbi Meir and Rabbi Akiva, both the sons of converts, that the convert is considered completely Jewish. This is why it is stated that even those who have yet to convert to Judaism were present at Mt. Sinai, at the moment of covenant. The peoplehood of Israel is only through the covenant which God made with those present at Mt. Sinai and with those who were there in a spiritual reality for God extended the bond of the covenant to them as well, and therefore even when the people were exiled from their land, and even when their blood intermingled, they did not lose the national bond (*ibid.*).

The implication of this is that the people of Israel is committed in all its generations through the covenant of its antiquity, by virtue of its being a people like any other, to its uninterrupted procreation and generation-spanning education; and by virtue of its commitment before its God which is a trans-historical commitment valid through-out the ages. This leads to a topical conclusion.

"He will gather in our dispersed from the four corners of the Earth — all of Israel is a brotherhood — and we will remain forever the people of Israel, and the stranger who dwells among us shall be as a citizen and will inherit a portion from among the tribes of Israel" (Ezekiel 47:22). As I explained above regarding today's pioneers, the *halutzim*, it is written, "Lift up your eyes and see how they have all banded together and come to you..." (Isaiah 49:18) and as is mentioned in many verses in the Torah and Prophets "no one shall be cast out from you" (II Samuel 14:14).

The words are used by way of hyperbole but there is a double meaning: those who are not religious are also members of the people of Israel, and as such the duty of the covenant applies also to them.

In order to complete the discussion of the notion of covenant as the basis for *halakhic* democracy, it is necessary to examine briefly two more issues. The first relates to the international commitments of the Jewish people. Rabbi Hirschensohn's view is that any international commitment has the force of a covenant. This is initially stated in the context of a discussion on the commandment, "You shall leave no soul alive," and the commandments relating to the conquest of Eretz Israel.

Although the *mitzvah* of conquering Eretz Israel is not limited to a specific time, as I explained in my book *Malki BaKodesh*, Part 1, there is no longer any *mitzvah* "not to leave a soul alive." Indeed, not only is there no such *mitzvah* binding on us, but we are prohibited from doing this, in order not to transgress against international laws which have been signed by the nations concerning behavior in war. God forbid that Israel might be considered among the peoples as savage or murderous, or to be acting against international law and the laws of civilization (*op. cit.*, p. 70).

The completion of this position into a cohesive approach comes in the discussion on the covenant between Joshua and the Gibonites.

It is indeed the opinion of our rabbis that even if a vow made with other peoples has been broken (by the other people) we must still observe it, in order to prevent the desecration of God's name. Regarding international law, because of the principle of avoiding the desecration of God's name so that non-Jews might not say that we are using technical minutiae in order to evade our responsibilities, we must not concern ourselves with legal technicalities as to whether the law was actually a vow or not (*op. cit.*, Part 3, p. 37).

The second issue relates to the internal character of Torah democracy. It is clear that this democracy affirms unity but the unity is a very broad-based framework, allowing for pluralism within it. It is important to appreciate that the covenant which establishes a people and legitimizes national legislation also validates the leaders of each part of the people — the tribes, districts and cities, "and other such parts of the public to make laws according to the situation of their particular sector of society" (*op. cit.*, p. 75). The broad framework encompasses different views, and the argument between these views is not merely legitimate, but is a positive basis for the covenantal regime which is inherently democratic.

Differences of opinion in a context of civility and rationality do not cause harm to the people. Just as the faces of different people are different, so are their opinions. In a parliament there are different opinions, but their political cohesion unites them. There should be alliances; this is our true salvation (*op. cit.*, Part 1, p. 166).

These words take on increased vitality when restated in the light of contemporary developments. Rabbi Hirschensohn encouraged the religious public not to withdraw from the World Zionist Organization but to remain within it as part of one grouping, despite differences of opinion. Naturally, they were not to abandon their separate outlook, but it emerges that they were equally obliged to respect other opinions. This democratic viewpoint is the basis of national unity.

Doubts and opposition only strengthen a situation once they have been settled; therefore in any civilized and constitutional country there are right and left wings in the parliament; only in dictatorships is there no opposition from within, merely an external opposition which seeks to overthrow the government sooner or later (*op. cit.*, Part 2, p. 57).

The issue is of great importance, and it is worthwhile summarizing the main points:

1) God did not impose His Torah on the people. It was offered freely and the people accepted it of their own free will.

2) The commitment to observe the Torah is a voluntary commitment on the part of a given individual.

3) After individuals have accepted a commitment to give up their self-interest, authority is vested in the leaders and representatives of the people to lead, legislate and enforce rulings.

4) The commitment of those who enter the covenant of the Torah is superior to the commitment of a "natural" people. The religious dimension penetrates the political dimension. It is expressed in the special responsibility that each individual in Israel has for every other individual in matters of the general good and in the eternal validity of the Torah constitution which is not dependent solely on continuity of territory or origin.

5) The ancient commitment maintains its validity throughout the generations and applies also to those of our generation who come within the "covenant of the people" and the "covenant of the Lord."

6) The authority of the courts rests with the public; "outside the power of the polity, the court has no power whatsoever."

7) Within the framework there is room for disagreements between the representatives of the people; the majority decision of the court is the definitive position.

8) According to the Torah, the people of Israel are obligated by those international laws which are accepted by all nations since these laws are of a covenantal character.

All these points serve as the basis for a topical discussion on the renewal of a democratic Jewish state. The sixth point in the list, however, is the basis for the immediate necessity of founding a state. Rabbi Hirschensohn understood this point as meaning that since the oath of the people to observe the Torah still stands, it is clear that when a Jewish public attains conditions which allow it to live a national life within the framework of a political context, it is immediately obligated by the commandment in the Torah to establish a national, political and legal system. Hirschensohn understood this point in two complementary aspects: the public obligates its leaders — wise men versed in the Torah — to lead the people in the *mitzvot* of the Torah; and the authority of these wise men to interpret the Torah, to make regulations in accordance with the Torah, to judge and to lead is vested in the people. The power of the people, acting within its limits, obliges the wise men to lead and obliges the people to accept their leadership — all this in accordance with the Torah.

Democracy is based not only on the commitment of free people, however, but also on the complete equality of all citizens before the law. Can the Torah constitution really be said to be democratic in this respect? The answer of Rabbi Hirschensohn is an unequivocal "yes." Above all, this applies with reference to the social regime. The Torah is opposed to any form of rule by one person of another to his disadvantage, and is opposed to any enslavement of one person to another. In economic terms, this implies not only the practical abolition of the institution of slavery, but also the abolition of any control of workers by employers. The employer purchases the labor of the worker; he does not purchase the laborer. The laborer by his labor acquires a share in the product, and this is his right, but he cannot abuse this right in order to control the property-owner who gives him work. Both sides remain free vis-a-vis the other, and the Torah lays down just guidelines for their mutual obligations. Indeed, Rabbi Hirschensohn attempted to define this principle of justice and to suggest a way for it to be applied in the social conditions pertaining in modern times.[2]

The principle of equality before the law is, however, of still wider and more comprehensive dimensions. The claim that the legislation of the Torah sees poor and rich, honored and humble, Jew and strangers in their midst as equal is hardly innovative. The real problem relates to the implementation of the democratic principle as understood in modern times in still another area, namely that of the status of women. Rabbi Hirschensohn dealt extensively with this question, in an attempt to solve it within the spirit of democratic equality.[3] Hirschensohn took great pains to stress the positive attitude of the Torah toward women and the honorable role it prescribed for women in the family, in educating children and in social life in general. There are also, of course, negative views expressed by the sages concerning women, but these reflect individual positions. The attitude of the Torah as a whole is positive, and women are not considered inferior to men; on the contrary, clear advantages are attributed to women and these are reflected in the unique characteristics which determine their significant role. Nevertheless, these comments are of no more than an introductory nature. In questions of substance, Rabbi Hirschensohn does not ignore the differences between the status of men and women in the lifestyle prescribed by *halakhah*; nor does he ignore the fact that these differences could be interpreted as an expression of legal inequality resulting from a perception that women are inferior to men. He utilizes to the full the opportunities offered by *halakhah* to draw closer to the modern democratic perspective, by proposing two important distinctions.

The first differentiation is between a *halakhic* principle and the decisions reached in response to the economic and political conditions of ancient life. The economic and political status of women in ancient society was a direct outcome of accepted norms in societies at that time. *Halakhah* adapted to that reality; it did not dictate it. In other words, a change in economic and political circumstances will lead to a positive change in the scope of activity of women, and *halakhah* does not represent an obstacle to such changes — indeed, it is open and oriented to them. What is required is a change in the social orientation of the Jewish public, not a change in *halakhah*.

The second distinction is between social and political status, on the one hand, and religious status, on the other. From the social and political viewpoint, the Torah grants men and women equal status before the law; from the religious viewpoint, it gives each sex a particular task. This is to be seen not as discrimination but as functional specialization. In order to explain this point, Rabbi Hirschensohn compares the difference between men and women in this respect to the differences between Cohanim, Levi'im and Israelim. In social and political respects, there are no distinctions between these three groups of Jewish men; the distinction is confined to the realm of religion and ritual. In Rabbi Hirschensohn's opinion, the same is true of the legal status of men and women. In this context, it is interesting to note that Hirschensohn also considers the acceptability of women to serve as witnesses in issues that do not concern assessments. A woman is as reliable as a man, and the distinction relates only to the legal procedure or trial which is an act of religious significance. It is true that in this respect *halakhah* differentiates between men and women for spiritual reasons not detailed in the Torah; this is also the case concerning the *mitzvah* to study Torah which applies to men only. The result of these two distinctions is that in the case of social and political differences, the difference between men and women becomes insignificant. Women are fit to vote, to be elected to public office and to be appointed to senior leadership positions in the political and social spheres. Women can also serve as witnesses in civil courts which center on assessments, and although the *mitzvah* to study Torah does not apply to them, they certainly have every right to an education which will develop and advance them and enable them to fill all their roles in the family or society.

Rabbi Hirschensohn thus succeeded in narrowing the theoretical and practical gap almost to the point of enabling legal equality as required by a consistent democratic perspective. "Almost" is the operative word, however, for the difference in the religious and spiritual realm remained. Hirschensohn based these differences on dissimilarities in mentality, and defined them not as discrimination but as distinction; nevertheless, this approach diverges significantly from the secular democratic perspective since the religious element does not — and, in Hirschensohn's philosophy, cannot — be confined to the area of ritual.[4]

This distinction between the social and political level, on the one hand, and the religious level, on the other, is also used by Rabbi Hirschensohn in explaining the difference between the attitude of the Torah toward Jews and the attitude toward Gentiles who obey the Noahide Laws. In principle, Hirschensohn insists, the Torah advocates complete social, political and moral equality between Jews and Gentiles, in the sense that any demand based on human morality applies equally to all. This is true of the *mitzvot* relating to charity and mercy — a Gentile who needs assistance is to be helped wholeheartedly, and in this case there is a definite prohibition against taking interest on loans from him. The difference relates to issues which go beyond moral duty, such as financial relationships where there is no moral objection to taking interest (viz.: cases when the interest is in fact participation by the lender in the profits of the borrower who borrowed for the purpose of making a profit). The different approach to Jews and Gentiles in such cases, according to Rabbi Hirschensohn, is once again based on religious and ritual considerations which do not in the slightest impinge on the full equality between Jew and Gentile in the eyes of the Torah.

It has already been noted that the constitution of the Torah is founded on the voluntary agreement of the public, for the good of the public, and on complete equality. It should be added that in Rabbi Hirschensohn's opinion, the Torah also maintains the principle of individual freedom of thought. It has been noted as well that the Torah does not make commandments relating to belief and opinions, and no thought that a person might have, even if it is opposed to the view of the Torah, is considered a sin or transgression; a man is not held to be the master of what he believes to be true. A certain ambiguity can be sensed in the thought of Rabbi Hirschensohn on this question, as on others. It has to be acknowledged that, along with the freedom of theoretical interpretation found in Torah literature, there are nonetheless limitations concerning the acceptance of pure monotheism and acceptance of the principle of Divine revelation of Torah, with all the ramifications of this belief. Even if we limit the extent of the prohibition, and see it as applying not to the thought itself but to the dissemination and teaching of heretical ideas, we are still left with a situation where the tolerance of the Torah does not match the concept of tolerance as understood in secular democracy. The nearest point that can possibly be reached — and this, as we see, only at the price of extreme daring which verges on a leaning toward opinions which have been considered of the utmost danger to Judaism — still leaves us on the other side of a border which, however much we limit its practical implications, is still fundamental and principled.

Despite the above difficulties, it nevertheless emerges that the political regime promoted by the Torah is essentially democratic. In a historical context, Rabbi Haim Hirschensohn does not deny that the leadership of Moses and Joshua was hardly democratic, but he offers a historical explanation for this. A people which has just left conditions of slavery is incapable of immediately accepting democratic leadership. The establishment of a nation-state never takes place in a democratic fashion — this is true of all nations, and was equally so of Israel; it is to be seen as inevitable and not to be condemned. Furthermore, the leadership of Moses or Joshua was far from what is considered autocracy; their leadership was designed to create the conditions and lay the basis for a national democratic regime. The claim is made solely to meet the needs of an historical explanation. Hirschensohn also drew a practical and topical conclusion from it. The Zionist leadership destined to establish a democratic Jewish state in Eretz Israel cannot itself be based on a democratic organizational structure. In its dispersion and given the lack of consensus regarding the establishment of a national state, the people are not ready for democracy. It is necessary to first establish a political framework. The goal, however, must be a democratic state in the spirit of the Torah. Indeed, during the period of Judges in biblical times, Israelite democracy was realized in practice, and became an historical reality.[5] Needless to say, however, this does not solve the problem.

The period of the Judges ended in the establishment of a monarchy, and one finds in the Torah the express *mitzvah*, "You shall appoint a king over you." In spite of Samuel's opposition to the monarchy, the monarchy of the House of David was ultimately sanctified so that over the generations the vision of redemption was associated with the reenthronement of the House of David in its ancient splendor. Does this not represent an obstacle to the introduction of a democratic regime on a par with the most advanced democracy of our time in the Jewish state?

This question was posed for the first time in *Malki BaKodesh*. It is inexorably linked with a second point relating to the ritual and religious side of the same problem: must Jewish sovereignty, acting in accordance with the Torah, renew sacrifices in the Temple? If so, does this not contradict in some way the spirit of enlightened democratic culture? Rabbi Hirschensohn's answer can be summarized as follows. There are two opinions in the Oral Law concerning the appointment of kings. The first view considers that this is not a positive commandment, but merely a restriction to be imposed if the people desire a king to be appointed. The second view does indeed see the appointment of a king as a *mitzvah*, but limits this to a particular historical function: the elimination of the memory of the Amalekites. Since this particular function is no longer relevant, even the second of these views would not demand the enthronement of a king in modern times. Hirschensohn also rejects the view that there is any particular commitment concerning the rule of the House of David. The people have no obligation toward a king whose rule has been interrupted, or to his descendants. As for the messiah-king whose arrival we await in the future, the intention is to some future time when human society will rise to a level of moral leadership which does not require external means of control. This is a distant reality, when the "king" will fulfill a function not of political or authoritative leadership but rather of spiritual leadership alone. The messianic idea does not have any bearing, therefore, on the nature of the political regime which should be established in the context of current reality — a political reality which is undoubtedly one of *redemption*, but is nevertheless in the context of a this-worldly historical reality. The principles of *halakhah* must therefore be applied in this situation and, as explained, these principles are unquestionably democratic.

Rabbi Hirschensohn adopted a similar line of thinking concerning the question of the renewal of the Temple service (centering on the sacrifices). It is true that we pray for the renewal of the sacrifices, but Rabbi Hirschensohn stressed that we ask that this be done in accordance with God's will. In other words, at the right time, God will show us what the correct form of worship ought to be; in Hirschensohn's opinion, this worship will be spiritual in nature, revealing the inner meaning of the sacrifices offered in the past. He based this on the opinion of Maimonides who saw the sacrifices as necessary at a particular point in history when all nations offered sacrifices to their gods. This was a concession made by the Torah to a spirit which prevailed among the people, and not an expression of "primary intention" on the part of the Torah. In modern times, no religion prescribes the offering of sacrifices, and it is unthinkable that precisely in this reality the Torah would do so. There would seem, then, to be an analogy between Rabbi Hirschensohn's attitude to the messiah-king and his attitude to sacrifices. Both these institutions will be discontinued as a revelation of ideal spiritual intent emerges from a former garb. In this context, it is important to compare the view of Rabbi Hirschensohn with that of Rabbi Kook, who responded to these ideas in a lengthy letter.[6] Rabbi Kook claimed that we should not be too eager to base our positions on the views of other nations, as progressive as these may apparently be. The morality and worship in the Torah are the fruits of higher spheres which the intellect of modern men cannot fathom. In the future, the worship (and sacrifices) will be reinstated in their literal sense and, in addition, the superior, genuine and truly progressive moral meaning of this worship will become clear to us. We will not have to take account of the opinion of other peoples.

In his reply, Rabbi Hirschensohn agreed that in messianic times we will be privy to supreme knowledge and will not stand in awe of the achievements of purely human culture; he also agreed that there was much hypocrisy and pretense in current moral positions. We must, therefore, strive to make greater progress in understanding the truth and the morality enshrined in the Torah which are certainly supreme; however — and this is the central point — "Knowledge and recognition will not regress, and lack of culture will not be considered culture" (*Malki BaKodesh*, Part 4, p. 8). In other words, the moral law which has consolidated in the consciences of the nations is of a lasting nature. The difference between us and them can lie in our progressing further on their achievements, not on our retreating into what they have already come to consider uncultured.

In any case, the result of the discussion is that, from the *halakhic* point of view, there is no difficulty in establishing a Jewish state with a democratic system of government; indeed, the Torah prescribes this and points in that direction. Rabbi Hirschensohn expresses this as a normative *halakhic* matter. Having already seen that we are not commanded in modern times to anoint a king over us, and that we have no commitment concerning the dominion of the House of David, Rabbi Hirschensohn now turns to explaining why the duty of "judges and administrators" does apply. This is an eternal *mitzvah*, and it is applicable to Israel as soon as the necessary conditions exist for it to be put into practice. This is because the commandment is based on the Torah and the democratic principle that the authority of leadership rests with the people. Thus, given the reality of a Jewish public in Eretz Israel free from the yoke of foreign rule, the leaders are required to establish institutions of law and order. These institutions are termed "judges and administrators." Rabbi Hirschensohn believed that in ancient times these institutions existed in a democratic form, and that we are commanded by the Torah to renew them, democratically, as soon as the conditions mentioned above apply. It should be emphasized that at this stage Rabbi Hirschensohn was referring to institutions of justice and legislation in situations relating to the leadership of the nation. The institutions would be elected by the people in the best democratic fashion, and this ruling does not, apparently, raise any *halakhic* difficulties. A more detailed study, however, reveals that this was not quite so simple a matter, and Rabbi Hirschensohn reflected on it throughout his work in an effort to find a positive solution.

The problem was that even though Rabbi Hirschensohn found no difficulty in presenting the political regime required by the Torah as democratic, it is clear that the democracy framed in the Torah cannot be identical to democracy in the secular sense of the word. A secular democracy is based on the sovereignty of human institutions in the field of legislation. A Torah democracy, however far-reaching the interpretative powers granted to the sages, and however binding the authority of the people over these sages, is nevertheless a democracy acting in accordance with Divine law and not in accordance with a human constitution. The implication of this difference as regards the political regime is the creation of a democracy different in its institutions and in its *modus operandi*. A sense of this problem can already be found toward the end of the first part of *Malki BaKodesh*.

Rabbi Hirschensohn appealed to his rabbinic colleagues to respond to his views with detailed arguments so that he could amass all the sources and all the possible interpretations relating to these questions, in order that the view of the Torah would be revealed. This was important because the purpose of the discussion among the sages was to *reveal* the view of the Torah; the choice of this phrase is far from incidental. Rabbi Hirschensohn was not seeking a consensus among the scholars concerning their views on these questions. He was seeking to extract the truth from the Torah, and he did not fail to make this distinction clear.

Rabbi Hirschensohn detailed both the Torah principle and its significance in terms of the democratic process: the well-known principle that one should "follow the majority" has a different significance for Israel than for other peoples. The goal of Jewish society is the spiritual well-being of the whole above the material well-being of some individuals. Spiritual well-being is based in absolute truth and justice, the supra-human knowledge whose source is the Torah. We are commanded to seek the truth with all our natural powers, but our finding the truth is dependent on Divine assistance. This truth is based in the objective authority of the Torah. How is this reflected then in the democratic process? Not only in the agreement of all those involved in the give and take of the ultimate authority of *halakhah*, but also in the way in which the majority is inclined. Only in matters of civil law, permits and prohibitions does one go according to a simple numerical majority in order to lessen the danger of disputes. In other laws, the decision is made according to the majority of evidence from the Torah supporting a particular point of view, and not according to whether a numerical majority supports that view. It is in this way that majority rule can be seen as devolving from the Torah and binding on those who study it through its objective truth.

In proximity to these views, Rabbi Hirschensohn attacks the lack of courage of modern sages in making decisions and innovations because of their self-denigration vis-a-vis the sages of earlier generations. The authority to make decisions was given to the sages of each generation. This view, however, does not change the basic understanding that what is being addressed is the discovery of the view of the Torah as it is understood by the sages of each generation, but not the unearthing of their personal views or the views of the public which they represent.

In the second part of *Malki BaKodesh*, Rabbi Hirschensohn deals in detail with areas which hitherto he had addressed in broader terms. In answer to a question relating to the authority of a supreme court to be established in Jerusalem and, in effect, intended to serve as a legislature for peace between religion and national life, he stated unequivocally that even if the authority to appoint judges and administrators rests with the people, the popular democratic principle that legislative and advisory institutions are elected by everyone should not be accepted. Those who understand the issues under consideration, in this case the Sages of Eretz Israel, are those who can represent the people gathered in the Land, and it is they who should elect the committee from among their number.

To avoid a misunderstanding, two restrictions should be mentioned immediately. Firstly, Rabbi Hirschensohn did not envisage this court as being empowered to deal with criminal law (indeed, he preferred the elimination of capital punishment, a step in line with the highest moral positions of our time). Neither would it be empowered to excommunicate any part of the public from the nation as a whole. The institution would have to accept all Jews, religious or not, as the basis of its authority and as falling under its jurisdiction.

The ramifications of this ruling emerge in the second restriction: the people as a whole are not devoid of authority concerning the institution which determines *halakhah*, and the sages must take into account all sectors with regard to the people's opinion as to what laws they feel they can live with. The legislator may not rule in such a way that most of the people will be unable to accept the ruling and, as noted, Rabbi Hirschensohn went so far as to support the abolition of many prohibitions which represented limitations because of the ambience popular in the modern era. Similarly, a regulation would

72

not apply unless it had spread among the majority of the people; if it had not, it would have no validity. In other words, Hirschensohn did not deviate in these respects from his fervent loyalty to the democratic idea although this is clearly a totally different concept of democracy, at least concerning the legislative and judicial institutions. As for the government itself and its institutions, these would be elected according to secular democratic norms. This becomes evident from his writings in *Eileh Divrei HaBrit* with regard to the authority vested in national leaders, as well as his views that full political equality must be granted to women. Hirschensohn refrained from proposing a detailed program for the institutions of democratic government, providing only a broad ideological framework.

A question arises which must be examined: what was Rabbi Hirschensohn's view about the practical resolution of the conflict between a *halakhic* democratic understanding and that of secular democracy? Was there a possibility that the non-religious Jewish population in Eretz Israel would come to accept, through democratic means, this *halakhic* version of democracy? The question is not only practical in nature. From the point of view of the *halakhic* Jew, it is a question of principle the answer to which throws light on the entire democratic outlook of Haim Hirschensohn. Hirschensohn himself argued that the people would have to agree to and accept the Torah as the basis of its political and social life. True, Hirschensohn never posed the question in its most *direct form*, but it is clear that it concerned him deeply.

On the basis of his writings, the following answer can be postulated: the obligation to live according to the Torah applies and is reinforced by tradition in each generation. This obligation pertains to the entire Jewish people, a proposition which Rabbi Hirschensohn did not see as arbitrary or undemocratic. His premise — true at the time he was writing — was that the religious public which accepted the Torah still represented a majority within the Jewish people, and certainly within the Jewish community in Eretz Israel. Rabbi Hirschensohn was well aware, however, that even in Eretz Israel there was a large and important body of Jews who were not religious and who were unlikely to see a *halakhic* framework for political life as something to be taken for granted. There would be no escape, therefore, from a dangerous confrontation, and in one of his letters he raised the possibility of failure which, for him, would imply the complete failure of Zionism.[7] Because of this possibility, he was not willing to forgo separate institutions for the religious public which had to ensure its future in the eventuality that it was obliged to act in isolation. However, Hirschensohn also saw a chance for success.

The question was, in what way would the two parts of the Jewish people, the religious-national and the non-religious-national, approach the conflict? If the paralysis in *halakhic* creativity continued, the non-religious public would establish its own civil courts and failure would be guaranteed. If, however, the rabbinic leadership showed an openness toward the whole range of national life, if it used its authority as a carrot and not as a stick, if it showed an understanding for the opposition of the national public which was seeking independence from the diaspora-like elements in *halakhah*; in short, if it fully applied the democratic principle according to its own understanding, there was a chance that the conflict would lead not to division but to a "peaceful war" — an internal struggle against a backdrop of national consensus which could end in a clearer crystallization of that consensus. In this way the *halakhic*-democratic framework of the people of Israel in its homeland could be saved.

The book *Malki BaKodesh* was written for this purpose, and the democratic aims of the book are expressed in two directions: in a call to the sages to recognize their obligations and authority and engage in the negotiation essential for the development of a *halakhic* framework for the future Jewish state; and in a call to the people as a whole to study *halakhah*, recognize its essentially democratic nature and, therefore, willingly accept its authority. These were the two conditions essential for the development of a national consensus. This would also seem to be the basis on which one should understand the consistent and frequent attention given by Rabbi Hirschensohn to such questions as the establishment of an appeals court in accordance with *halakhah*,[8] a *halakhic* adaption of the legal demands made by the British Mandatory government on the Jewish public,[9] and relations between religious and secular Jews within the Zionist movement.[10]

The first of these three issues was of particular importance, encapsulating as it did the claim of secular Jewish leadership that *halakhah* was inadequate for guiding modern civil life. Their goal was the establishment of a court which would rule in accordance with the civil law prevalent in Eretz Israel, an action which would entail a rupture in the legal framework determining the life of the

Jewish community in Eretz Israel. Rabbi Hirschensohn understood that the preservation of the common legal framework of *halakhah* was an essential condition for the emergence of a national consensus, and he therefore struggled against the creation of an appeals court outside the *halakhic* framework, preferring an attempt to maximize the possibilities of *halakhah* to answer the positive and legitimate demands of the secular national public.

There is a clear link between the views of Rabbi Hirschensohn concerning Jewish nationhood and his views relating to *halakhic* democracy. Democracy is based on the independence of the national base, founded in the will of the people per se; *halakhic* democracy is based on acceptance of the Torah as a "constitution" that is binding on the people and on their political and social leadership. The issue is not one of identity between the national and religious elements, but rather of a relationship between these two elements founded on mutuality. What would happen, then, if national identity were to break away from religious obedience? As noted earlier, Rabbi Hirschensohn retroactively recognized the emergence of such a situation in the diaspora, and aimed to maximize the ability of *halakhah* to relate positively to the national Jewish public which did acknowledge its authority. *Halakhah*, from its own perspective, would have to relate to the people in their entirety. If such a reality were to emerge in Eretz Israel, however, would *halakhah* be able to relate in the same way to a democratic regime; that is to say, a framework for complete national life which did not acknowledge it?

This is the question that remains today. Rabbi Hirschensohn did not answer it, nor, indeed, could he have done so. He was still struggling for the possibility that a different reality might emerge. Nonetheless, he expressed theoretical and practical problems in the clearest and most detailed way and, on the plane of principle and practice, his contribution in this respect is of the utmost importance to this day.

Notes

1. See *Malki BaKodesh*, Part 3, Question 1.
2. *Malki BaKodesh*, Part 3, Question A.
3. The principal discussion is in *Malki BaKodesh*, Part 2, Question D, although this issue is also dealt with in some important letters in Part 4, as well as in *Torat HaHinukh HaYisraeli*, Article 4, Part C — positions which were first expressed in print in *HaMisdarona*.
4. See *Torat HaHinukh HaYisraeli*, Article D, Sec. 2, Par. 4.
5. See *Malki BaKodesh*, Part 1, Question A.
6. *Op. cit.*, Part 4, first part of the letter.
7. *Op. cit.*, Part 6, p. 123.
8. *Op. cit.*, Part 1, Question E.
9. *Op. cit.*, Part 3, Question B.
10. *Op. cit.*, Part 2, Question C.

Chapter 7

SOCIAL AND CULTURAL PROBLEMS AND THEIR SOLUTIONS

An examination of the democratic essence of *halakhah* would not be complete, or even readily comprehensible, without developing a general rule of open-mindedness toward the full scope of Jewish national life, and its deliberate application under conditions of the modern era, so as to apply it in concrete detail. What, in actual practice, was Rabbi Hirschensohn's understanding of this rule of openness which he himself had laid down?

In an earlier discussion on basic principles, several issues were pointed out. Hirschensohn unequivocally asserted the equality of social and political rights for women under a democratic *halakhah* and narrowed down the difference in status between men and women to the domain of religion; similarly, he asserted that *halakhah* permits the appointment of a court of appeal for civil law cases; he pointed out ways within *halakhah* to adapt, or agree to, legal requirements stemming from the secular authority of an "external" (that is, not a rabbinical) ruling body if it turned out that such an agreement was vital for the Jewish public's national concerns; and finally he had the daring to propose that restrictions imposed by *halakhah* which the public could not live with, whether because of the force of existing circumstances or because of prevailing secular modes of thought, be annulled.

In probing the background to modern realities, however, further issues emerge, some of them pivotal and vital. The following discussion does not exhaust the full range of problems for which Hirschensohn suggested solutions within *halakhah*; rather, the main areas with which he dealt are illustrated by means of several of the most significant questions. It should be emphasized that while the specific solutions he proposed are important, they are not more important than the indication that they offer regarding his method for tackling entire areas of human interaction in the social and cultural life of a modern democratic nation.

In this context, the first field that bears looking into is that of the socio-economic clash between the working class and the class of property owners. Its intrinsic importance derives from its close link to the concept of democratic nationalism and the demand for social justice. To wit: if nationalism connotes the realization of a nation's internal freedom through the cohesion of its individuals, then inevitably equality before the law and social justice lie at its base. It is not enough for the people to elect its representatives and authorize them to rule. Each individual and each group need to take part in the election with that degree of independence and prosperity which belongs to all. This consistent link between nationalism and democracy, and between democracy and the idea of social justice — considered as a matter of principle — is an essential aspect of progressive and positive trends in the modern era; Hirschensohn understood this with great clarity.

It is characteristic of Hirschensohn's approach that, at the very beginning of *Malki BaKodesh*, he asserts that democracy — the highest achievement of political thought — subsumes a number of socialist principles, such as public ownership of land and property. The issue of the compatibility of *halakhah* with the notion of democracy is immediately dealt with in a broad context which includes the social question. The argument put forth at the beginning of *Malki BaKodesh*, Part Three, must be analyzed against this background.

Hirschensohn starts his presentation by setting out the historical perspective. In the past, the issue of the relationship between classes was "dormant." Neither slaves nor exploited workers rose up to claim their due. Enslavement and exploitation were considered tolerable conventions from the ethical point of view. Contemporary sensitivity to these issues must, therefore, be considered a sign of progress. Workers rise up and forcefully assert their rights, turning the social issue into a national question of the first order. It is important to stress that for Hirschensohn this was not merely a social or class issue; rather, it was a matter touching on the nation as such. It was an issue that needed to be resolved at the national level, otherwise the class struggle was liable to destroy national cohesion. Thus the essential link between affirming national democracy and social justice and basing class relationships on that justice was endorsed again. In any case, Rabbi Hirschensohn points to this question as a topical one that cannot be evaded.

At a time like this, we must reflect on how to order the affairs of our life in such a way as neither to labor for nought nor call forth panic; whether, as we base our political life in Eretz Israel, we should follow old and corrupt ways which others before us have followed or choose for ourselves new ways which may or may not be able to provide a remedy for our ills, ways which may be a road of life or which may lead us toward perdition: the ways of socialism about which there is doubt that they, or the theories underlying them, can exist in the real world (*Malki BaKodesh,* Part Three, p. 45).

Hirschensohn recognized the importance of the demands put forward by the socialist movement, but he did not accept the socialist solution, based as it was on a concept of class struggle. In his view, the Torah has a different answer, more suitable to the situation.

Indeed, let the daughters of Zion go forth and see what the Torah has taught. Look at the laws of the Torah whose ways are ways of pleasantness: neither by the sword nor the spear, neither in the tumult nor the thunder but only by pleasant ways. This applies as well to questions of property, of laborers and of commerce...that is, the welfare of the workers, the profit of property owners and the success of commerce. As to good laws for the regulation of trade, freedom of competition in commerce: whoever holds fast to the Torah will bring peace to all Israel. Amen (*op. cit.,* p. 46).

These are the words of an enthusiast, and at first glance they appear to be an apologetic idealization couched in general terms. But this impression changes as one proceeds to the purposeful *halakhic* discussion that strives for practical solutions. The question of principle here is: how does the *halakhic* approach, *as such*, differ from the socialist one? The answer stems from two claims of Hirschensohn's critique of socialism. First, socialism proposed to change the existing order by force but, Rabbi Hirschensohn contended, war never had any positive results and never would. By nature it was destructive, not constructive. Second, he himself proposed a new social order that had not yet been tried. It was utopian, for even though it was based on just principles, it was doubtful whether those just principles were applicable in the practical world. Hirschensohn did not give a reason for his doubts but it appears that two considerations were at work: the skepticism that necessarily attaches to every untried system, since a responsible leadership must take into account that the failure of an enforced solution may leave things in a worse state than before; and the surmise that it is a social order which ignored human nature because it aspired to establish a permanent order from which justice will necessarily emerge as if by itself, which means precisely that human reality is ignored in a most dangerous way. As against this, the *halakhic* solution, *as such*, is a model of practical idealism. It is not meant to uproot the existing social order, nor does it propose a new social order in its place. *Halakhah* always refers to a given situation. It has no ambition — at least not initially — to change the basis of existing socio-economic conditions; all it strives for is to circumscribe the social relations that exist between people as a result of those conditions, and to do so in accordance with absolute principles of justice and right.

Looking more closely at this point, one discovers the positive difference between socialist theory and Hirschensohn's *halakhic* approach. According to Hirschenshohn, the ills which need to be corrected do not flow entirely from socio-economic circumstances, nor does the good which is desired necessarily stem from socio-economic situations of a different kind. The principles of interpersonal relationships have their own independent status under any system of socio-economic conditions, and it is the network of these relations that must be addressed. True, this must be done by appropriately re-applying constant principles to changing circumstances, because to deal with interpersonal relations means dealing with real disputes between people and the causes of the disputes keep changing. But the *halakhist* does not, initially, attempt to change the overall framework of relations between individuals. He strives to change them within the system and he addresses himself to existing conflicts with the aim of finding a just solution for them. In doing so, however, he may contribute to a process which will eventually change the "natural" underpinnings of society. The *halakhist* must always asks himself what it is that a just decree demands in the context of its time. By setting forth what justice requires at a given moment, he can afford maximum satisfaction to all the conflicting sides and restore that peace which is vital to the success and well-being of the public.

With this consideration as his starting point, Rabbi Hirschensohn discerned three questions at three different planes: at the economic level, the question that was posed concerned the relative shares of labor and capital in the value of a finished product; at the level of social psychology, the issue was one of human relations between laborers and owners as human beings; at the socio-political level, the question was that of the overall responsibility of a democratic regime for the well-being of all sectors of the public together. Hirschensohn offered solutions for each of these questions, but for this discussion, rather than the solutions themselves, it would appear more relevant to observe the way in which he posed them and the principles underlying his search for answers.

The economic issue was presented by him as follows. Production, Hirschensohn said, involves two factors: capital investment in the plant and operating capital, and labor. The conflict between workers and employers originates in the question of the rights accruing to each side by virtue of its contribution to their joint undertaking. The correct solution is that which apportions just shares to each; it is predicated on the precise contributions of labor and capital to the product. It was Hirschensohn's view that *halakhah* provides an accurate yardstick for determining the share of labor in the value of the final product, and he sought to assess the worker's share in the profits of a factory in accordance with that yardstick.

The socio-psychological issue was a question of the human value of the workers and the employers in their mutual rapport. The conflict over this question focused on the employer's feeling that ownership of the plant gave him power over the person of the worker, and, conversely, on the desire of the worker not only to set himself free from such domination but to reverse the relationship altogether. The *halakhic* solution lies in denying the moral and legal right of both the sentiment harbored by the employer and the aspiration nurtured by the worker.

The conclusions of Hirschensohn's argument regarding the relative share of labor and capital in a product clearly indicate that he regarded workers and employers as partners of equal value in a joint venture. Though a difference did exist between them regarding their right to benefit from the plant's profit, in accordance with their share in the investment, their personal status was governed by the following maxim: equality based on independent choice and responsibility based on mutual obligation. Workers and employers joined the plant as independent persons and neither thereby gained power over the other. The employer bought the worker's labor, not his person; and the worker gained the claim to that part of the profit which corresponded to his share of labor in the product, but he did not acquire the employer's person or his property. They continued being free in their relationship to each other and their responsibility to each other. The practical significance of this argument becomes evident in the question of strikes. Hirschensohn argued for the unqualified right of the worker to strike if he felt exploited by the employer, for the employer had no right to coerce the laborer to work for him. At the same time, however, the worker did not have the right to cause the employer damage with regard to the latter's rights. If a strike caused damage in excess of that inherent in the very act of interrupting production, e.g., if at a certain stage it caused raw materials to spoil or led to damage of a similar kind, then the workers were to be held responsible, and the employer was entitled to claim compensation from them.

The socio-political issue was one of overall direction of the national economy. Hirschensohn acknowledged that under the conditions of a modern economy *halakhah* could not confine itself to defining what is just only in the relationship between workers and employers. This was because justice could not be detached from economic realities which were determined at the national level, if only for the reason that the value of the worker's wages depended on its purchasing power; therefore, if the purchasing power was not ensured, specific agreements in any particular plant were rendered worthless. It is here that one can see the extent to which Hirschensohn understood the far-reaching significance of the changes that modern conditions introduced into the system of economic relations. The development of industry and commerce permits civilization to prosper, but it also gives scope to severely destructive elements. In the absence of a restraining hand and of controls capable of imposing restrictions, economic prosperity can lead to economic disaster and the disintegration of the entire social fabric. Hirschensohn was therefore of the opinion that *halakhah* endorses government intervention for the purpose of restraint and limitation. The regime must not, it is true, suppress free competition in the economy, but it must control the overall price level and guarantee that a worker's earnings allow him to live at a decent standard of living, relative to his social environment.

Halakhic solutions therefore insist on justice being done at all three of the above levels: a precise determination of the respective shares of workers and owners in the profit accruing from their product; insistence on the independence of both, as free agents responsible for each other; and a fair measure of price control in the economy as a whole. Taken together, these three principles would lead to peace founded on justice and mold the several classes hitherto engaged in struggle into a united people.

Still another area with which Rabbi Hirschensohn dealt was that of the social ethos. It will be remembered that he touched on a series of related issues in his discussion of restrictions which the public could not live with. In doing so, he spoke not only of the difficulties which would obtain from running a modern state and economy, but also of the difference between the ethos of a free people living in its own country and the ethos of a people living in the diaspora. As circumstances unfolded, however, inevitably questions concerning the traditional Jewish ethos arose as a result of the broad social developments which typified modern times. In general terms, what is meant is the emergence of a society freer and more open in its interpersonal relationships, a society that transcends the organic units of the family and the small community. It follows that openness and liberty require a different kind of relationship which seems, at least initially, to be at variance with the patterns of social ethos which tradition formed under the conditions of a smaller, more closed society. This was bound to lead, on one hand, to the destruction of eternal moral foundations, and, on the other hand, to a zealous seclusion likely to end up in harming conservative Jewish society itself.

An interesting example of such an eventuality can be found in a chance remark of Hirschensohn's which was made in the context of his incisive treatment on the status of woman in *halakhah*. One of those arguing against him, Rabbi Hayim Mikhal Mikhlin of Jerusalem, wrote that Orthodox objections to women's suffrage, whether correct or otherwise, arose not only from considerations of *halakhah*, but from a defensive instinct. The Orthodox were not used to the rules and interplay of forces in a free political society. They were aware that the leftists were more adept than the Orthodox at turning these rules to their own advantage since that was the leftists' main business. Therefore the Orthodox preferred not to play the game. In short, seclusion was the result of the Orthodox defending themselves against a society which was truly out to do them harm. Hirschensohn's rejoinder was that Mikhlin's analysis as such was correct, but that it did not justify Orthodox reaction.[1] It was all very well to rely on instinct in circumstances which first shaped that instinct, but it was deleterious to react according to instincts formed under conditions that had since changed. Eventually, an instinctive reaction not checked by pragmatic judgment was bound to play havoc with the interests of those who react in this way. After all, the refusal of the Orthodox to let their women vote in elections reduced their electoral influence by one half. Similarly, their objections to setting up comprehensive schools for all — again, from a protective instinct — led to such schools being established without the Orthodox retaining any influence over them, thus turning them into bulwarks of opposition to religion. It therefore became clear that at the same time as efforts were being made to maintain essential religious concerns under the new conditions, even matters that touched on the fundamentals of ethos should be looked at rationally and adjustments made to the positive openness of life in a modern society.

An example of such a problem was a question discussed in Part Two of *Malki BaKodesh*: whether it is permissible for unmarried men and women to engage in teaching and education. There is an explicit rule in the *Shulhan Arukh* against employing single men or women in education, for reasons of modesty. But conditions of the modern era make their employment as teachers unavoidable. The science of education has progressed extensively, and teaching and education have become professions which need to be acquired at a young age, before marriage. To cling to the rule of the *Shulhan Arukh* therefore holds back progress in Jewish religious education. What, then, should the rule be? Rabbi Hirschensohn certainly did not belittle the concept of modesty, least of all in education, but, he believed, an enforced abstention from a contact which was an objective necessity of life, for no other reason than not to deviate from the merit of modesty, did not serve the real quality of modesty but rather that of hypocrisy. The significant thing, then, was that as a matter of principal consideration, the practical value of a procedure, or of some specific conduct, comes first. If teaching is under consideration, it must be considered according to the requirements of teaching. If something is good for Jewish education, then it is good. Only afterwards does one need to see to it that this good does not indirectly cause some harm, and it is quite possible to prevent that from happening. It should be carefully noted that Hirschensohn presented this attitude as the basic consideration that governed *halakhah*. The clause forbidding the employment of unmarrieds in education was not, in principle, a commandment but rather a piece of good advice. If, in the interest of good education, contemporary conditions offered cause to counsel otherwise, there was no *halakhic* obstacle against it. What, then, about the principle of modesty? That, too, had to be examined objectively. If one was dealing with a broad, open social framework which did not entail teachers and pupils being together alone, there was no need to fear that modesty would be transgressed against. The matter was therefore altogether permissible. Such was Hirschensohn's basic approach; his method was to inquire into the precepts that underlay a firm *halakhic* norm with the aim of maintaining the *halakhic* ethos in a new reality, yet without taking away from the positive values the new reality brought with it.

A third area that presented problems of this type was that of scientific and technological advance. Hirschensohn illustrated this in a response that related to the use of electrical appliances on the Sabbath.[2] Two elements contributed to bringing this issue to the fore. One was private. An American householder had turned to Rabbi Hirschensohn with a question about the use of the telephone on the Sabbath. He might, of course, simply not use the phone on the Sabbath. But to do so would cause him to face a moral dilemma: he had no way of knowing whether the caller meant to bring up a matter which could wait, or whether his call had to do with *"pikuah nefesh,"* a matter of life and death. Rabbi Hirschensohn chose not to reply in writing until he learned of a public dimension to the question: Pinhas Rutenberg was about to set up a power station in Eretz Israel. The introduction of an electrical network into the country would create a new reality. Was it feasible to expect the entire Jewish public to refrain from using electricity? Seen from the point of view of how to manage life in a modern Jewish state, this was a paramount question of national import.

The two elements which, together, occasioned Hirschensohn's reaction point to the principle underlying the question. For the individual — even more for the public at large — technological advance was no longer simply an auxiliary means for making life more comfortable, but a means for providing the infrastructure of society's way of life. This perspective was implicit in the way Rabbi Hirschensohn, without spelling it out specifically, posed the question as to whether abstention from the use of electricity was not liable to detract from the social image of the traditional Sabbath even more than the use of it. A *positive halakhic* solution was, therefore, imperative. Characteristic of Hirschensohn's approach, the vital necessity to arrive at a positive *halakhic* solution came first; the search for a legal way of finding it followed.

This was demonstrated most strikingly in a private letter he wrote to an enthusiastic questioner who wanted to persuade Hirschensohn to deal in a similar manner with other central issues.[3] In reply, Hirschensohn stated that there was, in actual fact, no question to which a positive *halakhic* solution could not be applied, always provided that it was brought up in an objective, detailed manner and in ample time. As an example, he referred to a question regarding the use of railways in Eretz Israel on the Sabbath, not entirely dissimilar to the use of electricity on the Sabbath. Hirschensohn was of the view that, all the difficulties notwithstanding, a rule could have been laid down if the *halakhists* had dealt with the question in good time. They were, however, tardy in considering the matter and, in the meantime, the prohibition issued by stringent interpreters of the *halakhah* had already taken hold among the pious. For Hirschensohn, technical considerations of *halakhah* (the distinction between igniting a fire which is caused by the combustion of carbon with oxygen, and the light and heat generated by electricity), though indispensable to the establishment of a rule, were not the essential element in arriving at it.

The decision to look for a positive solution came first, and it was based on a qualitative consideration concerning the value-laden goals of *halakhah*. Science and technology had created a new infrastructure for social existence, and the Sabbath was not intended to undermine that infrastructure. It may be assumed that those who created *halakhah* under the terms of the Oral Law would have related positively to scientific advance and would have seen its achievements, on its merits, as a positive fact. Did it stand to reason then that they would have refrained from conclusions affirming this or that aspect of change in societal existence brought about by such advances? So it was that in his detailed reply, Hirschensohn first of all dealt extensively with the attitude of the sages toward science, with the purpose of demonstrating that they took a consistently positive view of it. Indeed, their discussions of *halakhic* topics revealed a profound knowledge of the sciences of their period as well as an understanding that such knowledge was necessary to correctly discharge the problems of *halakhah* in their time. This *a priori* assumption served as the basis for legal and formal considerations of matters under discussion.

Rabbi Hirschensohn's attitude toward the achievements of scientific advance was at its most consistent and most daring in his reply regarding autopsies for the purpose of medical training or research.[4] That issue, too, became urgent in his view because of the new national realities which were emerging in Eretz Israel. A Hebrew University had been founded which was destined to play a pivotal role in the social and cultural life of the Jewish state. Without a doubt, the new university would in due course have a medical school and a medical research center. It was therefore imperative to move quickly in proposing positive *halakhic* solutions before the views of those who were stringent interpreters of *halakhah* became accepted by the community at large. In effect this would close the door to constructive, even vital, developments toward an enlightened public life in the circumstances and achievements of the modern era.

How did Hirschensohn approach the issue? First, he turned to an eminent physician who was not a *halakhist* but who was well placed as a scientist to attest to the need for autopsies in the training of doctors and in the advancement of medical knowledge. His testimony was unequivocal. There was no alternative to autopsies in teaching anatomy and pathology, and no medical student could be instructed properly without their use. As for research, the progress of medicine since autopsies were systematically performed outstripped several times the extent of medical knowledge achieved earlier. These premises served as the foundation on which Hirschensohn's *halakhic* discussion of the issue was based, for they pointed unmistakably to the need for a positive solution. In this instance, however, Hirschensohn's decision was also reflected in the discussion itself. He was critical of the rule laid down by Rabbi Yehezkel Ben Yehuda Landau, an eighteenth century *halakhist*, which later authorities took as their guideline for dealing with the question.

The rule of "*pikuah nefesh*" did not provide a broad enough basis for the required permission because it sidestepped the fundamental issue of the attitude of *halakhah* toward the prerequisites of scientific advance in the field of medicine — the moral value of such progress being beyond question. It was therefore necessary to take a substantive, rather than a technical, look at the central *halakhic* assumption regarding the issue of opposition to "disgracing the dead." What was "disgracing the dead?" What practices did the term connote? In examining early sources of the Oral Law, Hirschensohn arrived at a distinction between "respect for the dead" which touched on the very personage of the dead, in other words the eternal soul, and the "respect" those who survived and cherished one's memory felt in their hearts; the latter was a matter touching on the finite body as well. In this context, "disgracing the dead" did not refer to the dead but to the living and had its roots in the respect it was incumbent upon man to feel for life itself. If this was indeed the principle underlying *halakhah*, and if there was clear proof that autopsies were a life-enhancing need, and rooted in respect for life, then clearly the rule against "disgracing the dead" did not apply to autopsies. Hirschensohn acknowledged the need for limiting this overriding principle so as to show regard for different views no less well rooted in *halakhah*; but, without going into his argument in detail, it can be said that there was clearly a broad breakthrough in his conclusions which were based on both understanding the defined requirements of life and a definition of the moral principle of *halakhah*.

The inquiry into the above problem appears to illuminate Rabbi Hirschensohn's *halakhic* methods with respect to all issues. It was a method which did not start out *a priori* to change the interplay of a given societal and political system, but rather to address interpersonal relations within the scope of given possibilities so that eternal normative principles of justice and right might be applied to them.

In summing up, one can point to the conclusions which may be drawn regarding the application of *halakhah* in an era when radical changes in prevailing conditions shape reality. It is true that sometimes a new norm can be arrived at by applying an older one, but even then the resolve to seek a positive ruling based on considerations of principle comes first. This is even truer when formal treatment of an old norm does not insure a broad enough view for the positive solution which is sought. The proper way — the high road Hirschensohn chose in all his responsa — is to start from the religious-ethical attitudes that informed all traditional norms and to proceed from them toward a conclusion appropriate to the present time, while conforming to the moral and religious objectives of *halakhah*. This does not imply belittling former norms; quite the contrary, from the many-sided arguments that eventually led to the formulation of an old ruling, one learns the substantive views that shaped it.

This is, after all, the importance of historical inquiry in studying *halakhah*. This is how continuity and sequence are preserved in applying *halakhah* in the sense that today's *halakhist* must reconstruct the spiritual process which applies an eternal outlook to a norm that takes cognizance of temporal realities. If the *halakhist* concludes that social, political or cultural achievements are positive from the point of view of the moral and religious objectives of *halakhah*, in the broadest sense, then he will not recoil from changes in normative details, even if such changes appear far-reaching or outright revolutionary in their legal and formal aspect. Such is the full extent of the commitment of *halakhah* to the social, political and cultural basis of the Jewish people's existence.

Notes

1. *Malki BaKodesh*, Part Four, Response to Rabbi Hayim Mikhal Mikhlin.
2. *Op. cit.*, Part Five, Question 2.
3. *Op. cit.*, Part Six, Response to Rabbi Joseph Ben Zion, Bab"d.
4. *Op. cit.*, Part Three, Question 4.

Chapter 8

YISRAELI* EDUCATIONAL THEORY

Rabbi Hirschensohn considered his vocation to be that of an educator, and his literary work was meant to serve an educational goal. As part and parcel of his national-religious and democratic world view, education was not only his main instrument in helping to reach the goal but the very process of its realization. His book, *Malki Ba-Kodesh*, was intended first of all as an educational work for scholars, and through them to the wider public for reference and study which, in itself, would constitute a means for preparing the mind and heart for the practical changes that were needed.

It was therefore no coincidence that the book's only practical suggestion, to be carried out promptly, called for the establishment of an institution — parallel to the Hebrew University — to service the country's spiritual and educational leadership. The institution would mobilize religious Zionism's finest minds, providing a source of guidance and spiritual inspiration for the entire nation.[1] A careful examination of Hirschensohn's work reveals that he also envisioned an educational role for political and judicial institutions. For Hirschensohn, a democratic government, in the spirit of *halakhah*, meant an educating regime whose instrumentalities were primarily those of education rather than power. His constant preoccupation, then, with the issue of education is only to be expected. Indeed, he devoted a special essay, *Sefer Torat HaHinukh HaYisraeli*, to the subject.[2]

Hirschensohn's views on "Yisraeli" education were also an expression of his positive attitude toward the cultural progress of his day. Just as he reacted affirmatively to advancements in democracy, science and creativity in general, he also advocated the development of ideas in the field of education. He believed in embracing the achievements of modern pedagogy, adapted, of course, to the special

---

* Hirschensohn made a distinction between a Jewish ("Yehudi") and a "Yisraeli" education; it was very important for him. In this chapter, his generally preferred use of Yisraeli rather than Yehudi is maintained.

91

conditions, the sum and substance, of "Yisraeli" education. Not surprisingly, it was while grappling with contemporary educational problems that Hirschensohn became aware of the negative aspects, the weaknesses, confusion, and the processes of disintegration that were involved in adaptation to modern life.

In Hirschensohn's opinion it was possible to overcome these dangers. Nonetheless, among his many books, all of which are notable for their optimistic tone, it appears that *Sefer Torat HaHinukh HaYisraeli* has a quality of sadness about it, and though he did not believe that the generations were going from bad to worse, in this book he looked at the past with a wistful longing. Something had spoiled in the infrastructure of Yisraeli education. He was not certain it could be corrected in the diaspora and, given the very nature of the Hebrew public life that was emerging in Eretz Israel, he thought it rather unlikely that even there it could be corrected.

What did Hirschensohn see as the difficulties of education in Israel? An explication of the term "Yisraeli" education is helpful here. The use of the term "Yisraeli" was meant to lay aside, equally, the notions of "Jewish" education or "Hebrew" or "religious" education by those who insisted on these terms. The word "Yisrael" distinguishes the people from other Semites, who are also Hebrews, but it refers to all strata of the population, its various groupings and diasporas, as parts of one nation and it does not separate the religion as an element distinct from nationality in the educational process. The appellation "Yisraeli" totally expresses the Torah-national uniqueness to the outside world, and the all-encompassing unity within. But, as it transpired, a uniqueness and unity that could be agreed upon by the entire nation no longer existed.

The dichotomy in concepts of education expressed the problematics of education; it could be said that it already existed in the differentiation of the educational function, as a process in its own right, among other life processes of the nation. In the past, the educational process went along without special institutions, in the sense that the institutions of life — the family, the community and its establishments — were those that educated, whereas now education had become a separate issue. Indeed the isolation of education from other functions and institutions was a problem since, because of it, the various institutions of life ceased to educate.[3]

This was what Hirschensohn wrote in his survey on the history of Jewish education, a survey that was meant to bring a historical perspective to the discussion of what was taking place in his own day. According to that survey, it appears that only at a relatively late stage (the Second Temple Period) did special institutions for educating children begin to emerge, and only in recent times had this phenomenon taken on a defined and clear meaning, for even after the Second Temple Period education was carried on mainly in the general social institutions.

Something else in Hirschensohn's survey, however, something presumably more important, was indicative of the book's structure; that is, even after institutions for children's education began to be established, no special theory of education was developed. Thus a theory of Torah education had to be extracted from models embedded in the forms which had, for generations, guided the life of the nation. The implications of this statement vis-a-vis the structure and substance of "Yisraeli educational theory" will be examined subsequently; the more immediate question concerns the problematics involved in extracting and developing educational theory as a separate issue: the fact that Yisraeli education had ceased to be all-encompassing because it was no longer directly anchored within the totality of the nation's life.

This question bears examining in detail. Hirschensohn saw three problematic areas in Yisraeli education: 1) the disintegration of the nation's unifying national foundation; 2) the penetration of materialism as a supreme goal and measure of success in life; and finally, 3) the decline of parental authority and the gap between the children's and the parents' way of life and values. The three factors were connected or, at the very least, re-enforced each other.

The disintegration of the national foundation was, of course, a result of the Emancipation. Community and family frameworks were weakened and neither one was a sufficiently forceful factor in education. Hirschensohn dealt with these components at great length, however, in relationship to other areas. In the present context he pointed in particular to two phenomena: new, external contents that were in competition with the contents of Torah education, and the dominance of certain foreign assumptions embodied in these new contents that subsequently prevailed over Torah education. Ostensibly these are two stages of the same phenomenon, but they need to be dealt with separately, if only because Hirschensohn had a different response to each of them.

Hirschensohn noted that initially a young Jew should acquire a broad "general" education alongside the Torah study which hitherto had been the exclusive educational pursuit of the Jew's spiritual life. The ideal of the scholar (*talmid hakham*) who dedicates all his life to Torah learning was difficult to achieve and very few attained it, yet even these singular few would lose all influence over the people if they lacked a basis in the common knowledge which people learned and lived by. It was a grave problem, not because the new contents were of a bad quality — on the contrary, as noted earlier Hirschensohn related to them positively — but because Torah learning, as shaped by previous generations, indeed demanded total dedication. Thus, if study of the Torah were to be pursued as it had been in the past, there was little chance for a youth of average talent who was also studying in a general school to reach a high level of knowledge, let alone internalize the essence of Torah learning. Moreover, even if he succeeded in learning something and internalizing the educational values of the Torah, a dichotomy would exist in his spiritual life for there would be no internal connection between the values of the Torah and values learned elsewhere. Therefore, while Hirschensohn had a positive attitude toward the achievements of modern culture and was ready to devise a system of Torah study which would allow enough time to attain a necessary general education, and though he saw the integration of a world outlook and life experience as an indispensable condition for education, he nonetheless felt that the very condition of integration was endangered by the apparently mechanical replacement of Torah education by "general" education — even granting that that education, in and of itself, was of a positive nature.

The second phenomenon, though stemming from the first, presented an essentially new situation: the danger that national-cultural values whose origins lay outside Jewish culture, and which constituted the basis of creativity in language and science, would become dominant and displace the national-religious basis of Yisraeli education. The danger was much more palpable in the diaspora, exposed as it was to the direct social and cultural influence of the environment. Instead of Jewish values providing the matrix for a new Jewish cultural synthesis, European or American cultural and national values might virtually invalidate Yisraeli's unique heritage. Clearly, if Hirschensohn's response to the former phenomenon was to search for a positive way to integrate Jewish and general elements, his response to the latter phenomenon was a singular effort to protect national-religious education from any such danger.

Hirschensohn's discussion on the replacement of a Jewish value-base by a foreign national value-base may appear too general, but it has a particular meaning, first of all, with regard to language.[4] In Hirschensohn's mind, the struggle between cultures focused on the competition between languages: between Hebrew as the language of Yisraeli education and Gentile languages. The Jewish value-base, he sensed, would be pushed aside if Gentile languages became the language of education. More specifically, it was not only that language bound the members of the Jewish nation together and defined them from others, it was also the means through which the child, from a very early age, internalized the contents and values of his national culture, as well as a belief system.

The Hebrew-speaking child understands the foundations of Jewish religion — including elements which appear difficult — in a simple and unmediated way; a childlike way, perhaps, but nonetheless a correct one because the sources are open before him and he can relate to them directly and experientially. This is not the case for a child who does not know Hebrew, who then needs historical and theological explanations which, in all likelihood he will not understand. Foundations of faith and the maintenance of the way of life it requires are laid in the early years. In other words, not knowing Hebrew is a barrier between the child and the spiritual world of the Sources and whatever he may learn later through intellect can never compare to that which he acquires as a direct experience. Furthermore, the delicate primary bond between nationalism and religion is woven on the plane of the Hebrew language. Shunting Hebrew aside means shunting aside the encompassing and unifying national matrix, with the resulting displacement of the spiritual-religious values that bind the Yisraeli people to its national foundation as a flame is bound to the coal.

The replacement of Hebrew by a foreign language is not the only manifestation of this phenomenon. No less tangible is the superficiality of a Jewish lifestyle[5] in which, along with a higher cultural content, the customs and style of the foreign heritage penetrate into Judaism; when the language at home is foreign, the circle of alienation is complete. Even if the parents were consciously religious nationalists, the home atmosphere would not be directed along a clearly defined path so it could not provide the basis for guided, unmediated educational and learning activity. Hirschensohn saw this as the primary source of all the difficulties.

Focusing on the second problem area, it must be said that the external factor displacing Jewish aspects was not simply foreign nationality. It was secularism as well. Here, again, it must be emphasized that Hirschensohn's relationship to the concept of secularism was not that of conventional "Orthodoxy" which is predisposed to simplistic rejection. While it was true that the secularism with which Orthodoxy came into contact was often grossly materialistic, there were also positive aspects, especially in the realm of individual morality. The problem was that even the positive aspects caused difficulties in education. As to secular materialism, the more a youth dipped into it the further removed he was from religion.

Indeed, even when such a youth recognized the values of religion, he did not live by them. Though this was a widespread phenomenon, there was a still more serious difficulty. A youth who is separated from the substance of Torah as it is expressed in the Hebrew language and maintained by the fullness of a Jewish way of life will quickly discover contradictions between the positive moral values of the familiar secular culture that surrounds him and the dullness of what it was he managed to comprehend in his childish study of Torah.[6] In other words, in light of secular conventions much of the Torah will seem strange and unattractive and this will only increase his sense of alienation. In the past a Jew who knew the Torah by virtue of daily observance could naturally and without difficulty use interpretations handed down from generation to generation to bridge the differences between his own moral understanding and the literal meaning of the Torah. However, for the person who has cut himself off from that continuity, for whom the Torah is no longer authoritative, the tools necessary to bridge these differences are not available. He is alienated. And the positive values in secular culture, rather than encouraging a new integration with Jewish values, create misunderstandings about the inner meaning of Torah.

The third problem area, the distance between children and parents, may be attributed to general societal processes of the modern era, but it was accelerated in contemporary Jewish life. Initially, it was actually the parents who were distanced from the children because parents did not invest enough of themselves in their children's education. In part, this stemmed from a preference to direct their efforts toward material attainments, and in part from an inner flagging of belief and adherence, by the parents, to the Torah and its *mitzvot*. This was true as well for those religious Jews who became lax in their religious observance so that they failed to adequately demonstrate in their own lives that which they would have liked to transmit to their children. Parents wanted teachers to provide their children with what the parents themselves were not capable of giving them directly, but clearly this was not possible. Moreover, the teachers were usually not unlike the parents. This being the case, children became detached from the parents' way of life. If, then, the parents overtly attempted to retrieve authority through punishment or dogmatic rigidity, their actions only caused the children to rebel, intensifying the estrangement.[7]

It should be emphasized that this analysis focused on that Jewish public that wanted to give its children a Yisraeli education. It was in the comportment of this group — not only in that of the assimilationists, whether religious or nationalist — that Hirschensohn uncovered the weakening influence of secularism. No longer simply a disturbing factor which penetrated a sector of the Jewish public, secularism had become a widespread phenomenon in modern Jewish society.

How did Hirschensohn deal with these problems? It has already been suggested that *Sefer Torat HaHinukh HaYisraeli* contains a note of sadness, perhaps even of despair. Hirschensohn had proposed an approach that seemed to him to be favorable, even attainable, but the picture which emerges regarding the attitude of most parents and teachers leaves the impression that he did not trust the parents to act as they should. Neglect was increasing even within the religious public. There is room to assume that his hopes centered on Eretz Israel, and that this book was written mainly for Eretz Israel. There too, of course, success was not assured by public life alone, but a strong national will prevailed in Eretz Israel and that raised his hopes.

Hirschensohn's first and basic requirement did seem certain of being fulfilled in Eretz Israel: educational institutions there would deal with Yisraeli education in the totality of their program, and not just as one course in the curriculum.[8] Hirschensohn did not mean by this that an educational institution should teach only Torah studies — he clearly considered general studies to be important for their own sake. He believed, however, that the unique elements of Yisraeli education should also be reflected in those general subjects which fashioned one's world outlook. With this in mind, he suggested that special textbooks on all subjects be compiled for Jewish schools; these would be produced according to the finest techniques of modern pedagogy and would enable all the schools to be guided toward the same value-goals and breadth of national culture.

Beyond any doubt, Hebrew should be the language used between parents and children, and between teachers and pupils. The same held true for diaspora communities. The importance of Hebrew was emphasized in Hirschensohn's writings from the outset of his work as an educator in Eretz Israel. Much of his effort was dedicated to the preparation of textbooks, the development of a teaching system, and an explanation of the importance of Hebrew speech as the basis of a national-religious Yisraeli education. The language of the Jew must be Hebrew, and not just as the language of prayer and Torah study. National education should encompass a person's life in its entirety; thus speaking the national language was the prime requisite, though it was not less important from a religious standpoint.

The connection of religion to nation is reflected in the language. Hebrew speech creates the context between the daily unimpeded experience of Torah and *mitzvot*; it interprets daily life in terms of the Sources. Thus even matters which were difficult to understand and which required a great deal of maturity and education would be comprehensible to a child as the immediate content of life. It is Hebrew speech that unites national life with religious life and ensures that they complement each other; on the other hand, separating the language of "religion" from the language of culture cuts religion off from its national fullness and empties it of its uniqueness and vitality.

Clearly, Yisraeli education would not take root if parents did not recognize their total responsibility toward their children's education. Mothers and fathers are the primary educators, and they must continuously accompany their children (not only in infancy) in this educational role. The obligation continues throughout the time that close and vital contact between parent and child exists. Nor does the task end when children become parents themselves; the educational obligation applies also to the children's children.[9] Obviously, the form that education takes changes from age to age, insuring that children are not deprived of their independence (a point that Hirschensohn was careful to make even with regard to early childhood).

The main point, however, is that the very relationship between parents and children is one of education, a concept Hirschensohn derived from *halakhah*. It is an obligation and a *mitzvah*, and the *halakhic* obligation turns the parents' educational activity into something which is both instrument and content in the sense that the very existence of the educational obligation, even before considering its content, is that of educating. It is an obligation to impart the generational link of the heritage to the consciousness of children. Unity and the continuity of the link between generations are the basis of national life, and they are the basis of a life of Torah and *mitzvot* in which commandedness is inherent. Accordingly, a parallel can be seen between Hirschensohn's ideas concerning the relationship of parents to children and his ideas about the Hebrew language: the national foundation is also the religious foundation, thus there is no religious education, in the sense of Torah, without a foundation which is shaped by the quality of the relationship between the generations.

There is a juxtaposition in the performance of parental obligation to educate their children and the type of education that exists within the family. An indispensable condition for rehabilitating Yisraeli education is that the parents ensure the preservation of the *mitzvot* and the Torah way of life at home. In this way of life, content is directly transmitted; it also enables parents to educate, not by coercion which never succeeds, but by instruction which reenforces children's freedom and independence.

If, as noted, the obligation of parents to educate is a means which is manifested as content, then it can be said that the Torah way of life at home is content manifested as a means. The way of life must be organized and directed toward education; that is, its manifestation is education even if its meanings are self-evident. Thus it is necessary to guide the religious way of life at home so that not only is a routine created, but attention is aroused and interest and thought stimulated. The child who is stimulated to ask about the meaning of things he sees and experiences gives his parents the opportunity to be properly educating parents, which means that the parents can then relate and explain. And, since the questions arise on a background of living experience, it is certain that the answer will be understood for it is a decoding of existing, tangible matters linked to feelings and senses which the child can correctly comprehend.

In any case, the obligation of the parents works itself out by their having created the opportunity to educate, by telling their children the story of the nation's history (which is at the very foundation of the way of life), by explaining the meaning of the *mitzvot* and customs, and by guiding their children in ways of "mussar" which, according to Hirschensohn's definition, means order or proper disciplined human behavior. Though they respond by talking, teaching and guiding, in actuality parents must educate by example; it is in this way that their educational responsibility is brought full circle. The school's integrative activities build on this education and further it.

These are general requirements and, along with other requirements necessary for rectifying Yisraeli education, they need to be internalized. Hirschensohn placed great importance on the readiness of parents to explain the meaning of the *mitzvot* which he felt to be of special consequence in the present generation.[10] Under the influence of what is accepted in the culture of the day — ipso facto positive — children are not ready to accept every norm of behavior as self-evident; vague answers such as, so we have been commanded to do, are not acceptable. Indeed, children tend to rebel against such answers. Thus even when referring to *mitzvot* which have no specific meaning, the general meaning which is at the basis of the *mitzvot* must be explained.

Moreover, when explaining the meaning of *mitzvot* and the principles of faith to a child, care must be taken not to say such things as the child cannot understand from within the personal experience of his milieu. Dogmatic statements cause a warped understanding or bring about rejection. One example, which Hirschensohn paid particular attention to, elucidates what he meant.[11] How does one explain the idea of personal providence in reward and punishment to a youth raised in today's cultural ambience? There is a definite tendency among ultra-Orthodox educators to preach and threaten along the lines that certain punishment will surely be meted out to transgressors. Indeed, this is done concerning the *mitzvot* between man and God. Aware as these educators are of the excessive apathy in their environment toward the *mitzvot*, their intention, which may be good, is to see to it that their pupils observe the *mitzvot* out of a "fear of heaven." So they threaten them with immediate punishments from heaven.

In most cases, however, results are just the opposite. Social experience teaches youth that there are many who transgress the *mitzvot* and come to no harm. The effect is a total loss of respect for belief in providence, a basic principle of the Torah. The approach

Hirschensohn proposed is typical of his thought. (This becomes even clearer in the section on theology.) It must be emphasized that, in actuality, the issue of direct reward and punishment applies to the moral realm, where the result of evil is immanent in sin, and reward immanent in the good deed. This can be seen by youth from their own life experience and by its accord with moral values that are generally agreed upon. The element of historical observation also comes into play: a glance at the history of the Jewish people as a nation discloses the truth of the notion of providence in which every Jew, as a member of his people, has a part: the Jewish people survived only through full observance of *"mitzvot."*

In a like manner, Hirschensohn counseled parents concerning the intelligent way to use authority in dealing with their children.[12] In many instances, parents themselves caused children to rebel against the entire Torah way of life when, in the name of the Torah, they forced their children to act in an unjustified manner. In the certainty that they were right, the children, not unnaturally, regarded the demands of their parents as proof of the parents error and consequently as a condemnation of the entire Torah way of life. Thus parents needed to be cautious in what it was they demanded, using the authority of the Torah only when they were perfectly sure of it. But if they came to the conclusion that they had to demand a certain authority, then it was necessary that they demonstrate, by their own behavior, a resolve that testified to their conviction of the justice of their action and its real importance for themselves, not only for their children.

Hirschensohn believed that in most cases children were inclined to honor their parents' wishes out of genuine concern. They had, he felt, the sensitivity to distinguish between a demand which stemmed from religious rote and a sober demand which, if it was not fulfilled, would cause the parents sorrow, not simply because their authority had been violated. Parents needed to weigh matters carefully before making demands to insure that they were justified and that their children would have a similar assessment. According to Hirschensohn this required a certain amount of Torah learning without which no Yisraeli education, or Jewish way of life, was possible. In order that they might properly educate them, parents had to be capable of *halakhic* discretion in their relationship with their children. Thus learning penetrated into daily life, and the question of punishment was brought to the fore.[13]

It was Hirschensohn's belief that one must be very careful about punishment and that past the age of *bar mitzvah*, punishment must be avoided completely because at that point parents no longer carried the responsibility of their child's "transgression." Which meant, as he understood it, that parents were then free of the obligation of punishing the child. Indeed, punishing past this age was a sin since the mature child might then react in a way that could cause him to transgress the commandment of honoring one's parents. Such a result was a grave sin, and parents who provoked it were in part liable for it. However, he allowed for a certain educational measure: parents of grown children had only one obligation: to continuously educate. The obligations of support and economic responsibility ended when the child reached *bar mitzvah*.

Thus the father might be impelled to present his children with the alternative that if they wished to study Torah he would continue to support them out of his obligation to educate them. If, however, they did not wish to study Torah, they would have to support themselves, and in effect, that decision also became a way of educating. In any case, the rule of Yisraeli education precluded overly authoritative and harsh guardianship for it would only drive children away rather than bring them close.

In the teaching of Jewish Sources, Hirschensohn was exercised by two grave questions. The first concerned Scripture. How does one overcome the contradiction which exists, at least on the surface, between the accepted authoritative moral judgement of the surrounding democratic culture and the behavior of some biblical characters?[14] The question arises in the modern era not because the moral level of this generation is higher, but because the previous generation, immersed as it was in studying Torah and finding its total authority in the configuration of its way of life, did not let these contradictions come between it and Torah. They immediately interpreted contradictions according to their received Torah learning, in its entirety. Such is not the case for someone of this generation whose approach to Torah, from the onset, is external. Thus the contradictions appear before the person who has not learned sufficient Torah to be able to deal with them from either an overall Torah understanding or a historical perspective.

Since this is the situation, some sophistication is required of today's educator who must prevent those he teaches from being confronted with contradictions before he has given them ample knowledge with which to deal with them. At the outset, a basis of identification with the Sources must be created. Afterward, pupils will themselves seek solutions for the difficulties and complexities, at which point the confrontation with awful acts which go against morality will not only not cause harm, but will help in the pupils' spiritual and moral development.

Hirschensohn, therefore, held that it was absolutely permissible not to teach Scripture in the order set out, and it was also permissible to skip over problematic matters, so long as each scriptural section dealt with was taught completely. He went so far as to suggest beginning the study of Torah with the Book of Exodus, first because it does not raise any awful problems and second, because in his view, the story of Israel's exodus from slavery to freedom and the giving of Torah is indeed the beginning of Jewish education. (Genesis, he saw, as chiefly a narrative interpretation of the *mitzvot* of the Ten Commandments.) The issue of the teaching of Scripture in relationship to biblical criticism will be dealt with in a separate chapter since it refers to students at more advanced levels and is intimately connected with a theological discussion of Hirschensohn's thought.

The next question in teaching Scripture touched on the way in which the Oral Law should be taught.[15] Though essentially a matter of methodology, it was one of preeminent importance. The Oral Law is the fundamental element of the national-religious way of life. Without a basic and encompassing knowledge of the Oral Law, or, even more far-reaching, without the independent ability to think along *halakhic* lines whose substance is the application of *halakhah* that springs from an understanding of the process in which it is learned and adjudicated for the reality of renewing national life, no Jew is able to live a Jewish life as it should be lived. This applied not only to outstanding scholars but to all Jews; its application was not simply as concerned "religious" ritual *mitzvot* but also, and perhaps mainly, in the realm of morals, as in the issue of education itself. In exercising parental authority parents needed to think in a *halakhic* manner and, as will be shown, for Hirschensohn this was a basic characteristic of Jewish morality.

Where common sense is called for, a Jew must be capable of acting justly toward others in decision-making matters. For this one needs knowledge, an understanding of the systematic fundamentals of *halakhic* thought and the skills of *halakhic* thought. Many years of Torah study are required to attain this level yet, as has been noted, this was not possible in the new circumstances of the modern era.

General studies were also important for Torah scholars if they did not wish to be closed off from the life of their society. In addition, every Jew needed a profession in order to earn a living, and this required basic study and training. Was it, therefore, possible to decrease the amount of time invested in Torah study without doing harm to both the scope and quality of knowledge? Preoccupied by this question as early as the years in which he founded *HaMisdarona*, Hirschensohn had by then formulated his methodological answer both along the lines of Maimonides and of a university curriculum.[16]

The modern university succeeds in training students in complex subjects within the period of a few years. Why could not something similar be done in the area of Torah instruction? The advantage of the university lies in its use of a scientific systemization which is absent from the study of the Oral Law. By teaching rules and principles along with examples, the university is able to encompass a wide range of detail within the generality. The study of Oral Law, on the other hand, is carried on in a thick forest of detail, and only after he has amassed great quantities of minutia does the student arrive at an understanding of the principle. It was for this reason, to provide time for the study of science and philosophy alongside Torah study, that Maimonides, in his *Mishneh Torah*, wanted to change the system.

Hirschensohn acknowledged that Maimonides' solution was valid for students who had reached a certain level in their knowledge of the Oral Law, but he believed that modern circumstances dictated the use of a scientific method of instruction from the very first stages of learning. In one of his first essays, *Sefer Mosdot Torah Sh'b'Al Peh*, written in 1889, a methodological textbook for the study of the Oral Law, he had already suggested such a method. The first part of the essay deals with questions and answers between the rabbi and the student; definitions of *halakhah*, its essence and the subjects it deals with; and an orderly systematics of *halakhah* which branches out from main sections to their components. Care was taken throughout to employ at least one main example for each section in an attempt to explain the material inductively. The second part of the essay is a collection of talmudic issues with commentary by Rashi, an issue for each of the topics dealt with in the first section.

Hirschensohn wanted both parts to be studied in tandem so that the systematic study would not be dogmatic. Moreover, along with a survey of the logical structure of *halakhah*, students would be entering into a *halakhic* give-and-take, thereby acquiring the fine skills of *halakhic* thought. The book is a combination of two methods of learning, deductive and inductive. In this way, Hirschensohn thought, knowledge of the part would include knowledge of the whole so that even if the ordinary student did not learn tractates of the Talmud in their entirety, he would have a close knowledge and an overall understanding of the Oral Law. Still more important, he would be able to examine any *halakhic* matter he wished to since he would possess the tools to do so. For more advanced students, Hirschensohn proposed a selection of the Tosafists. It must be emphasized that the book was meant for instruction in the first stages of studying the Oral Law; it was not his intention that eminent scholars be educated only by this method. For them, the traditional method was also necessary.

Hirschensohn's intention was to insure that the education of every Jew would be minimally at the crucial level required for maintaining the Torah way of life. Of course, he believed that the progress of higher Torah education could continue according to a similar, though much broader, pattern. In his book, *Sefer Beirurei HaMidot*, he made note of and explained the theological, logical and juridical principles of the Oral Law, and developed rules of thought in a detailed, systematic manner with the intention of guiding and facilitating the study of outstanding scholars.

In examining the above material, a number of principles that Hirschensohn garnered from modern pedagogy can be identified. From the scientific standpoint, it was the need to suit the level of studies to the level of the child's understanding at every age, to make tangible and to foster the direct experience of the child, and to systematically graduate the structure of the subject studied. From the aspect of democratic character, Hirschensohn took from modern pedagogy an opposition to external, coercive discipline, severe punishment, unbending dogmatism, and the encouragement of independent understanding and thought. These principles appeared to him to be fundamental to Yisraeli education.

HaHinukh HaYisraeli was actually constructed as an aggadic and *halakhic* interpretation of those chapters of the Sources that deal directly with the role of parents and teachers in educating children. These are the Pesah Haggadah, a model of the father's instruction to his children; the Proverbs of Solomon, which Hirschensohn calls "Hinuch HaHinuchim" (analogous to "Shir HaShirim," the "Song of Songs"), "the quintessential education" of Solomon and is the model of moral education; and God's word to Abraham, "For I have singled him out, that he may instruct his children and his posterity to keep the way of the Lord by doing what is just and right..." (Genesis 18:19). Though the study of both *halakhah* and principles are nourished by the entire treasure of Torah literature, this verse he saw as the basis of moral education.

In the introduction to his book, Hirschensohn advances a short precis (which at first sight seems dogmatic) of seven fundamentals of Yisraeli education: 1) love of God and dedication to God; 2) love of Torah learning and observance of the *mitzvot*; 3) feelings of love and justice, including general human morality and love of the nation and its heritage; 4) belief in the special providence of the Jewish people, the choseness of the people of Israel and the miracles which were done for it; 5) the narrative of the giving of the Torah and the obligations it involves; 6) belief in the individual providence of reward and punishment in accordance with the understanding that fulfilling a *mitzvah* is its own reward; 7) fear of God in the sense of awe of His exaltedness.

An examination of these seven fundamental bases discloses that they are not immutable principles in the sense of Maimonides or Joseph Albo. They do not provide the basis of a binding theology and their formulation is not of an intellectual nature. Numerous times, Hirschensohn expressed the opinion that the Torah does not demand particular beliefs and opinions. Is there a contradiction here between this and the assumption that faith in the providence of the Jewish people (especially the giving of the Torah) and individual providence in reward and punishment are essential foundations of Yisraeli education? From a formal standpoint it does seem to be pressing the point somewhat, but Hirschensohn was unaware of it because it was not his intention to teach an unequivocal dogmatic principle. The Torah does not have a binding theological interpretation. It does give clear guidance concerning the behavior exacted by the *mitzvot*, and the development of characteristics and emotional-psychological attitudes.

Thus it should be noted that instead of a dogmatic formulation of belief in one God, etc., there is a formulation which channels psychological tendencies: love of God, love of Torah, feelings of morality and justice, fear of God, etc. The emphasis on the relationship to the Jewish people as the essential content of education is not accidental. It is the combination of religious education and national education that moderates the tension between the obligation to affirm formal foundations of faith and the opposition to dogmatic instruction.

Education, even if it guides toward certain views, is not in the realm of indoctrination; it does not act directly on thought but on a sense of belonging to the nation whose common ground is the unique social-historical life experience. Put differently, the essence of religion is acquired through a positive relationship to the nation's way of life. In any case, Hirschensohn's concept of education consistently assumed a vital connection between religion and Jewish nationality.

This assumption explains the distinction Hirschensohn made in the four different "types" of education: psychological, practical, narrative and instructional.[17] By psychological education he referred to the feelings that rise in a child growing up in a home that is distinguished by its Jewish way of life. This is a foundation given without any specific design, as a routine. There is no coercion but neither is there any choice involved on the child's part; he is simply part of the totality to which he belongs. But that is insufficient. Within the family structure, the child's attention must be aroused to the extent that he wonders and asks questions without calling into question his self-understood sense of belonging.

There is, of course, purpose and meaning to this approach. The arousal to wonder and question, as a positive phenomenon to be encouraged, is the beginning of education directed at the psychological, experiential level, and it is followed immediately by practical education. Parents must encourage the child to ask questions, and their answers must offer explanations and be tolerant. They need to be patient even when the stimulus to ask questions reaches the natural psychological level of contrariness and rebellion. From this standpoint, even the question of the wicked son in the Pesah Haggadah is an inseparable part of the educational process. A practical response is required: the way of life in the home must encourage the child not by preaching but by example. Hirschensohn explained this by comparing the Festival of Sukkot to the Festival of Pesah from the point of view of educational activity.[18] Pesah demonstrates how the question is stimulated through the process of identification, and how it should be answered. Sukkot shows how to motivate for action, and how the action is itself a kind of statement. If the action of parents raises questions, the child, by participating in the action, understands and identifies with it, and thus discovers the answer. Narrative education unites the first two. Parents tell the child stories that are the background to the way of life at home; in this way the child acquires a historical perspective, not as something abstract and distant but as something living that touches him in the here and now.

Hirschensohn cautioned against combining psychological, practical and narrative education with instructional education because, as it appears, he considered them opposite disciplines. Psychological, practical and narrative education are directly connected to daily experiences in the Jewish home, whereas instructional education deals with a subject-discipline. The child sets out on a course of new spiritual activity, one that differs from the usual routine and progression of the narrative, into a course of theoretical study. A mix of two disciplines such as these can be detrimental. If psychological and narrative education become instructional, they are of no benefit. If instructional education turns into narrative-experiential education, neither would it be effective. On the other hand, these methods should not be totally isolated from one another. The story is the transition to instruction and it creates the motivation to learn, while the study of Torah is guided toward living experience because it deals with life issues and because it creates habits of thought which help the Jew to deal properly with his experiences.

As noted, Hirschensohn used the festivals of Pesah and Sukkot to help him explain the nature of education in the family when the children are young. In guiding those about to become parents themselves, Proverbs was useful in the explanation of how to set up a suitable home for their children, and the model for instructional education, used by the teacher or the school, was the give-and-take of *halakhah*. There is, however, another kind of education which appears to connect instructional education to the encompassing totality of daily life — moral education.

Where does moral education fit into Hirschensohn's thought?[19] It is difficult to give a simple answer. Hirschensohn does not begin with moral education, except as it directly pertains to the people in a way of life marked by the performance of *mitzvot*. When, however, he deals with the rules of morality between man and man, he appears to see it as the very root of education from both a religious and a national standpoint. From the religious point of view, doing good deeds and acting justly is to walk in the ways of God. It also guarantees maintaining "the image of God" in man.

As a species, man is exalted above all living things in that man is concerned about others and tries to do good for others, something which the other animals do not do because they are concerned only with themselves. In this, man is in the image of God in that whatever God does is for the benefit of his creatures, and when man tries to preserve the way of God to do good deeds and act justly with others, "beloved is he who was created in God's image" (*Sefer Torat HaHinukh HaYisraeli*, p. 167).

From a national standpoint, the fraternity of the nation is expressed in the interpersonal moral commitment between the individuals of the nation, which is to say a covenant. This view, however, does not subsume religion in morality, neither does it subsume morality in religion. The closeness to God brings satisfaction to the person who walks in the ways of God, performing good deeds and acting justly as God has commanded him to do. This view does not simply assert a subjective experience; it is expressed in a way of life. *Mitzvot,* including the *mitzvah* of worshipping God, enables the partnership between people within the community of Israel, and it is inconceivable that morality should displace worship, or overshadow its importance, just as it is inconceivable that it would overshadow national belonging. The totality of religious-national life is the subject of morality, and morality is its vehicle. Each type of education has its own function: moral education begins with psychological and practical education at home; it continues in the instructional education of the school, and consolidates them.

Hirschensohn understood the ideal of Jewish moral education to be a balance between the extreme religious charge to worship God, or the essentially extreme demand to walk in His path, and the humanistic view which sets man as the measure of morality. It would appear that here, too, there is an attempt to respond to the positive ideal of modern humanism which is manifested in democracy while at the same time preserving the uniqueness of the religious view. According to Maimonides, the whole man is required to emulate God in His attributes, and His attributes are the rules of His behavior as the Creator of the Universe. Hirschensohn disputed this definition.[20] In his judgement, it not only transcended man's capabilities, but even what is appropriate to him.

God acts with a measure of extreme lovingkindness. He does not negate the right of the criminal and transgressor to live even during the moment of the crime. This is a sublime attribute which is not permitted to man. Human society can be maintained only if punishment is meted out during the period in which a crime is committed, in order to save the victim. Thus walking in the way of God deals with behavior that God set down for man in His Torah. It is not the qualities of God during Creation that are the ideal for human behavior but His ways with people according to the testimony of the Torah. It is evidently in this contraction that one sees a humanization of the religious ideal. Man, his human capabilities, and his needs as a social creature are all measures of morality. The step which follows immediately after the contraction, however, is a step toward expansion. In his book, *Eight Chapters*, Maimonides recommends walking the middle road. All extremism, including extremism in being good to fellow human beings, is a degree of piety that exceeds that which is required; it is permissible in only a limited way and within defined circumstances.

Here, too, Hirschensohn disagreed with Maimonides. Hirschensohn believed that the Torah teaches that each person is commanded to act according to a measure of piety greater than that of the golden mean. Charity is not a matter of free volition, it is obligatory; that is the meaning of walking in God's way. Man approaches God in that he recognizes that lovingkindness, an attribute of God, is his absolute obligation. In this respect it is not man who is the measure of moral behavior, it is God. However, this is within the limits of the example God sets for people, not for Himself. In this way the concept of charity is made into a construct of moral-religious education, and it is indeed a construct in the sense of an obligatory *halakhic* ruling: *halakhah* posits that the act of charity is normative. Educational activity is expressed in the effort to shape the inclination to charity in a manner which will suit itself to a mandatory norm.

This is the basis of the distinction Hirschensohn makes between charity and benevolence.[21] The difference between these two concepts is not measured either by the scale of the deed or the gift. It is measured rather by the human manner in which the act is carried out. By itself, charity is an act performed out of obedience to a mandatory norm, while benevolence is a deed enacted out of love of others, expressed by the human relationship, the warmth and the psychological encouragement attending the deed. In other words, charity is a system of conduct stemming from an obligation; it is education that must fill it with human content, the content of love. Here, again, the balance is found between the constriction of human capability, and the expansion which corresponds to the religious requirement of love.

The aspiration to find a balance between these two criteria, human constriction and religious expansion, may be observed as well in the solution proposed by Hirschensohn for the tension in the *halakhic* relationship to non-Jews. How is the apparent partiality in *halakhic* obligations toward the Jew, as distinct from the stranger, to be explained? According to Hirschensohn, the human obligation of the Torah applies to all people; there are not two types of justice, nor are there two types of obligations which are concerned with helping the Jew and helping the non-Jew; but there is a difference between them from the standpoint of religious obligation. The Torah demands more with regard to the Jew than is required by the humanist measure.

Hirschensohn examined this distinction in the circumstance of interest on loans which Jews are forbidden to take from other Jews but may take from non-Jews. He believed that interest on a loan which had been given to save someone from distress is forbidden in any case; the textual source discusses business loans made for profit. There is nothing morally wrong in gaining benefits from such a loan, and it is permitted from the viewpoint of human obligation. But a Jew is forbidden to take interest from a fellow-Jew for religious, not moral, reasons. It is worth noting here what Hirschensohn wrote about the uniqueness of "a covenant of the people" which becomes refined into a "covenant of God": the fraternity of the nation, anchored in the covenant made before God, creates obligations which are higher than the human moral measure.[22]

Charity, at any rate, is the purview of the ideal moral relationship to people, while justice in Hirschensohn's thought is a course that educates toward charity. The concept has two meanings. In its constricted meaning it relates to a judge's dealings with two litigants; in this sense justice is dispensed by an expert in defined moral matters. The second meaning, however, is broader and relates to every Jew. Each person must train himself to continuously judge his behavior with others; when a problem arises in his relationships, he may not act out of habit or instinct but must weigh in his mind what is just, carefully examining his and his fellow's rights.

Actually, this is a continuation of Torah scholarship entering into the hustle-bustle of life. The give-and-take of a talmudic discussion that is meant to arrive at a Torah truth is not just a manner of study, it is also one of conduct, shaping the moral thought which guides everyday behavior. In this sense, study becomes a behavioral discipline. Hirschensohn interpreted the term "mussar" (moral) in this connection, not as moralizing or rebuking (*yaser, yissurim*) as it is usually understood, but as the binding of morals (*mossrot*), or a discipline relating to human behavior.[23] Thus morality is a system which limits and defines human actions concerning others and society, and in this sense it is identical with a broadly conceived justice. The intent here is not to a system of norms that are set, *a priori*, for every action, but to a system of normative principles that all people must learn, along with the skills to apply them in various situations. The moral person is one who objectively judges each situation in which he is subjectively involved, in order to determine what is just both for him and others. It is this objective relating to the "I" and the "thou," without the relationship between them becoming externalized and cold, that Hirschensohn characterizes as the moral personality of the Torah scholar.

All the principles of the Oral Law and a great part of the written Torah constitute the science of deeds. For the Torah of the heart and the mind can encompass, in a few words, the concepts of justice, wisdom and morality, of knowledge and fear of God, etc. The very foundation of morality is that a person recognizes, feels and infers the particulars of these principles. Performing moral acts in accord with tradition and commandment, but without feeling, is not in accord with the Torah of morality which is basically a feeling and understanding of the heart. Even the Torah of deeds must be felt and understood not as a religion of rote, for that applies only to its affinity with an accompanying Torah of morality. Inherently, its main thrust is the correct and the just action (*Beirurei HaMidot*, Part One, p. 179).

That is to say, "justice" is the path to realizing the ideal of "charity." The moral feeling of loving others is the motive force, but the deed by which this is expressed is a complex wisdom requiring constant learning, and practice in application. This juxtaposition joins the personal motivation to be kind to others with the objective consideration which determines at any given moment what is best for that moment.

Notes

1. "In Lieu of a Preface," *Malki BaKodesh*, Part Two.
2. The book, written in 1925, summarizes a lifetime of teaching and educational experience (published in Romania in 1927).
3. See *Sefer Torat HaHinukh HaYisraeli*, Second Essay.
4. Language instruction was part of Hirschensohn's work from the beginning. Aside from his textbooks, his essay in *HaMisdarona*, Vol. 2, "A Tactic to Enrich the Hebrew Language," should be mentioned. From the educational standpoint, he dealt with the topic in *Sefer Torat HaHinukh HaYisraeli*, Second Essay, Ch. Four.
5. *Ibid.*, Third Essay, Ch. Four, Sections Three and Seven.
6. *Ibid.*, Chapter Four, Section Two.
7. *Ibid.*, Fourth Essay, Ch. One, Section Two; Third Essay, Ch. Two, Section Seven.
8. *Ibid.*, First Essay, Ch. Two.
9. *Ibid.*, Third Essay, Section Four.
10. *Ibid.*, Third essay, Ch. Two, Section Two.
11. *Ibid.*, Fourth Essay, Ch. Two, Section One.
12. *Ibid.*, Third Essay, Ch. Two, Section Seven.
13. *Ibid.*, Fourth Essay, Ch. One, Section Two.
14. *Ibid.*, Third Essay, Ch. Four, Section Two.
15. *Ibid.*, Ch. Five.
16. See *HaMisdarona*, Vol. One, and *Sefer Mosdot Torah Sh'b'Al Peh*.
17. *Sefer Torat HaHinukh HaYisraeli*, Third Essay, Ch. Two, First Section.
18. *Ibid.*, Third Essay, Ch. One, Sections One, Two and Three.
19. Essay Four of *Sefer Torat HaHinukh HaYisraeli* is devoted to this question.
20. *Ibid.*, Fourth Essay, Ch. Two, Section Two.
21. *Ibid.*, Section Three.
22. *Ibid.*, Section Four.
23. *Ibid.*, Ch. One, Section One.

Chapter 9

THE ISSUE OF BIBLICAL CRITICISM

The subject of biblical criticism engaged Rabbi Hirschensohn's attention more than any other theoretical issue posed by modern culture. He dealt with it on both the *halakhic* level — was it permissible to employ the method of biblical criticism while teaching in institutions of higher Jewish learning[1] — and on the research level. He searched for a solution that would allow one to comprehend the internal problems of the Bible, and believed that in order to be true to the Bible and *halakhah*, such a solution needed to be in consonance with the system of the Bible itself.[2] It was not surprising that the area of biblical criticism should hold Hirschensohn's attention so forcefully. If, *a priori*, one affirmatively viewed the achievements of modern culture in the scientific field, then the issue to be confronted was that which called into question one's entire religious outlook, for this was the question that posed the most direct and crushing attack on the very foundations of Judaism from the standpoint of scientific thought. What was astonishing was the daring and consistency of the solution Hirschensohn proposed, a solution which did not relinquish either freedom of scientific criticism, or faith in the principle of Divine Revelation.

In reconciling the relationship between the truth of prophetic revelation and philosophical truth, Hirschensohn's method paralleled that of Maimonides, embodying a further development in the procedure of Rabbi Nachman Krochmal's interpretation of the Rambam. According to the Rambam, one had to first determine the basic truth which was at the basis of each of the existing instructional sources, and afterwards examine how they correlated with each other. Hirschensohn saw no reason to doubt the reliability of the tradition which testified to the giving of the Torah to the Jewish people through Moses; that is, the belief that the Torah was the word of God received through prophecy by Moses from God and transmitted to the people of Israel in written form. For Hirschensohn, this was a first incontrovertible truth. Denying it, wholly or in part (such as an assumption that not all of the Torah was received by Moses through prophecy from God),

115

was a denial of the entire Torah and a person who taught in this way had no place in the Jewish faith.

A second established truth was that the Sages of the Oral Law were the only persons authorized to pronounce decrees, according to *halakhic* methods, on every issue concerning the practical precepts. Indeed, there is a valid, established *halakhic* ruling that one should not change the accepted written version of the Torah as it had come down to us through the generations. Changing or amending the written text thus denied the Oral Law which, in turn, meant that biblical criticism based on assumptions contrary to these two truths was totally forbidden, and Jewish research or instructional institutes were forbidden from dealing with it.

On the other hand, scientific research is a science. It is based on critical methodological principles, for the purpose of clarifying historical facts and drawing logical conclusions from those facts. In its own field, science was sovereign. Without getting involved in the question of what *halakhah* is, because *halakhah* is a separate discipline, it should be noted that inherent within this statement was the notion that the binding rule of *halakhah* was arrived at by methods other than those of scientific inquiry and therefore it could not be questioned in the name of conclusions drawn from scientific inquiry! One has to comply with the fact that in the area of scientific inquiry, "the demand for historical truth is the ruling principle, and there is no authority in the world before which the demand for truth bows" (*Yamim M'Kedem*, pp. 235-236). In studying the Torah and all the biblical books, every researcher was permitted — even commanded — to understand the written text in the light of its inherent meaning, to the best of his ability, and through the consistent use of research methodology. If there were difficulties, such as internal contradictions between one passage and another, or lack of continuity of texts, not only was it permissible for the researcher to raise questions and study them without restraint, it was his obligation to do so. Moreover, he was obligated to investigate questions that arose from knowledge whose source was outside the Bible.

Hirschensohn, of course, was of the opinion that if one avoided facile generalization and understood precisely the foundations of the truth of "religion," on one hand, and of science, on the other, there was no conflict between them. On the contrary, they complemented each other. The determination that the entire Torah was given in written form by Moses, who received it through prophecy from God, did not mean that the version of the written Torah extant today did, in fact, transmit God's word to Moses in the self-same order of books, sections, sentences and words, nor did it mean that there could not have been an error by those who copied the words; the determination that the version of the Torah extant today was holy according to *halakhah*, and for *halakhic* use, did not mean that it was forbidden to interpret differently on the assumption that within the written text there had been a change in the sequence, or even a transposition of versions. The fundamental belief was that Moses did not put down anything that was of his own thought, but that each and every word he wrote in the Torah was a prophecy from God. The primary point of the *halakhic* ruling was that it was forbidden to change even one iota of the *written* version. But everyone was permitted, indeed obligated, to interpret Scripture according to the truth as he saw it, even to a change in *his reading* the sequence of sentences and passages, or the version itself. Indeed, in this sense it was also permissible to disagree with the interpretations of the Sages for interpretation as such had no *halakhic* authority.

The distinction between freedom of interpretation according to scientific principles, on the one hand, and the binding authrity of *halakhic* determination, on the other, can be seen from Hirschensohn's writings on the issue of biblical chronology. Here the student was faced not only with very serious textual difficulties, but also with a question regarding the very authenticity of the dating of creation from the point of view of the scientific researcher, followed by a question of the correctness of the accepted chronology according to *halakhah* from the point of view of history. Hirschensohn did not hesitate to determine, quite simply, that the dating of creation did not begin with the creation, nor even with the "first man" (who was not a historical persona), but with the beginning of historical memory, and that the chronology as set in *halakhah* was not a historical chronology, but only a *halakhic* convention. As such, it was indeed obligatory, but only as such.

> I have already explained in Essay Two that nothing can gainsay or contradict our reckoning and counting; just as the exact date is noted in a divorce document, just as our reckoning is not a geological one, as I explained in Chapter One, it is also not a chronological one, but a religious or literary accounting only, according to the calculations of the author of *Seder Olam Rabah*

(*The Greater Chronology of the World*), Rabbi Yosi ben Halafta. There are even Sages who wrote articles disagreeing with Rabbi Yosi and, according to their method, the number of years in reckoning the history of the world was different. Nonetheless, our counting from creation is arrived at according to the reckonings of Rabbi Yosi....Whoever differs in his reckoning of the time of creation, though he may be closer to historical truth, yet he disregards the counting of the Jews from Rabbinic times because they agreed to count according to Rabbi Yosi, the Tannah. This indeed was his established status: the *halakhah* is always according to Rabbi Yosi's ruling, even where it concerns the practical *halakhah*, and even when he ruled against his friends, indeed even when there were more Sages who supported his antagonists than those who supported him...for it is obvious that *halakhic* rulings such as these are not concerned with uncovering truth, but concern themselves only with indeterminate issues on which it was impossible to arrive at a definite, clear knowledge of truth, while an agreement was necessary for *halakhic* reasons, so they decided to rule unanimously according to the views of that Tannah who was considered wisest and most authoritative. But of course this should be taken only as concurrence and not as a conclusion of scientific research (*Yamim M'Kedem*, pp. 240-246).

To summarize: one must distinguish between the belief that everything that Moses spoke was prophecy from God and the determination that the formulation of the writings extant today is exactly as was told by God to Moses. One must also distinguish between a *halakhic* decision which was in accord with its own unique considerations, and the search for historical truth. If one believed that the Torah of Moses was divinely revealed, and that *halakhah* was an obligatory authority for practical life, broad opportunities opened for historical, philological and critical research in which there was no limit whatsoever by any authority. Indeed, Hirschensohn used this door of opportunity which he himself had opened so widely, and his suggestions regarding a critique of the authenticity of a given version of the Bible were quite far-ranging. Hirschensohn believed these suggestions would be an important contribution to reinforcing faith in the Torah and obedience to *halakhah*. His opinions on this issue were close to those of Rabbi N. Krochmal: since historical criticism had greatly developed and had become generally accessible, it was, in every respect, desirable to support its positive and convincing achievements and thereby prove that the holiness of the Torah and the authority of *halakhah* were valid.

In Part Two, Question 6, of *Malki BaKodesh*, Hirschensohn defined the limits of what was forbidden, what was permissible, and what was commanded concerning the issue of biblical criticism: a person who studied Torah as if there were no Torah, i.e., as if it were the words of flesh-and-blood people speaking their own minds, was a thoroughgoing heretic. On the other hand, a person who studied Torah as Torah and erred in his understanding, was not a sinner and was to be considered worthy for upholding the precept of Torah study. The rule for the study of Torah as Torah was that it was permissible to assume that a specific word as seen today was not as Moses wrote it, or that one might read it differently than the tradition, or that the sequence of events as told to Moses was different than the order now extant, as long as one did not change the written text itself. Moreover, historical research for its own sake was useful, and study of the Torah in the light of historical knowledge was desirable.

These considerations served as the basis for a detailed *halakhic* ruling, the study of which indicates just how forceful the attempt was to expand positive areas and limit forbidden ones, beyond even that which would seem to be derived from previous considerations. This was done by the addition of a *halakhic* categorization which differentiated sections within the prohibited areas, detecting in them a certain degree of license. The categorization was delineated as completely forbidden, exempt but forbidden, exempt and allowed, commanded. Accordingly, a complete ban was placed only on that class of critical study which assumed that Moses had himself composed something and declared it in God's name; however, even the assertion that certain verses, not his, were inserted into Moses' utterances was not totally forbidden. Such an assertion was, at any rate, an admission that God spoke to Moses, denying only the reliability of the transmission. The critique was thus both exempt and forbidden, including emendations to the accepted written formulation.

From that point on, permissible was divided into two: exemption and permission to interpret the Bible in consonance with "its own integral spirit," even by means of comparing formulations and emendations, but on condition that one did not emend the written version itself (unless citing the emendation as a suggestion in research or interpretation); and a requirement to study the rules of the masoretic text, the depth and breadth of Hebrew grammar, the rules for expounding the Torah, and research into the concept of historical progression. Consequently, a broad-scoped biblical inquiry which used critical philological methodology would be permitted according to *halakhah*, and a Hebrew university study would not be limited, for the ideas of those who deny the prophecies of Moses should be studied as well in order to know "what to respond to the heretic." It should be emphasized that analysis such as this applied to university studies. In teaching Bible in elementary schools to children and youth, all of these methodologies were to be avoided.

But Hirschensohn was not satisfied with merely determining a *halakhic* position. He formulated an interpretive, critical and methodological viewpoint of the Bible which he applied down to the smallest details, and devoted four very important essays to the subject. *Yamim M'Kedem* dealt with questions of the chronology of the Bible; *Seder LaMikrah* dealt with the question of the original editing and rendering of the Bible and suggested an annotated version; *Eileh Divrei HaBrit* was a historical study on the development of the covenantal idea in the Bible; and *Nimukei Rashi* was not only an explanation of the interpretive technique of Rashi, but the formation of an independent, interpretive approach to the Bible which took into account the outlook of the Sages.

In all these monographs, an examination of Hirschensohn's approach discloses his consistent application and development of the distinction between scientific historical criticism and the interpretation of Oral Law. At the same time, he suggested a common basis in the Bible for these two approaches, each so different from the other. This, indeed, is the difficult question which the reader must determine: how can two approaches so removed from one another, even if not in direct contradiction to each other, converge to form one point of view? To assess the depth of Hirschensohn's convictions on this issue, it is necessary to dispel a mistaken understanding as to the place of historical research in his method. From what was previously said, the impression may have been imparted that while Hirschensohn considered historical research legitimate and upheld its assumptions and methods without compromise, from the aspect of a traditional interpretive outlook, it was, in fact, an external component. That would be a mistaken impression. On the contrary, Hirschensohn believed that there was an internal Torah value to a precise historical understanding of the biblical testimony.

The Bible was a historic work, written with the intention of testifying about historical events, and as such it had a permanent value as the basis for the belief and lifestyle of the Jewish people.

And every narrative which is written in the Bible, be it of the most wondrous marvels and miracles, is not a parable but simply a recounting of the history and events in the life of our people. Because the Bible is both a historical narrative and a religious book, and the indication of this is that it affords most of the miraculous deeds a natural cause: which only means that the natural cause was vouchsafed by God, Who accomplishes His deeds through His angels, and His servants are winds and fire.[3]

It should be emphasized here that Hirschensohn's meaning was that the Bible was a historical narrative in the modern scientific sense. If one of the conditions of scientific history was that it accepted as true only naturally possible events and not miracles, Hirschensohn showed that the biblical story stood this test as well, and that alongside the theological dimension which interpreted certain events as a miracle, there was always the natural dimension answerable to the tests of scientific history. It was characteristic, then, that in the continuation of the excerpt quoted above, Hirschensohn went on to suggest the historical significance of the collapse of the walls of Jericho, and the historical non-miraculous significance of the sun and moon "standing still." As in the Rambam's method, Hirschensohn thought the true measure in biblical history was the prophetic dimension which linked all the events in Jewish history to the idea of providence. In addition, not only did Hirschensohn understand all the biblical stories as straight-forward historical accounts, but he believed that one was obligated to teach them as such to the people so they would understand the depth of the narrative's significance, especially from a religious viewpoint. In his interpretation of Jacob's words during the vision at Beit El that if God would stand by him, God, who is revealed by His Name, would be his God, Hirschensohn remarked:

I dwelled on this at length because it is something which stands at the pinnacle of Judaism; people pass over it casually, they say the name of God thousands of times when they read the Bible, and repeat it in their prayers. Not only do they not understand its philosophical mystery — which not everyone can understand unless they study diligently and have a deep, direct knowledge of philosophy and Kabbalah — but they do not understand the historical point in it, for lack of knowledge about the ways of ancient peoples, their thought and feelings. These points shed light on the historical aspect, if not in all its details, so that a "wise man might hear and increase in learning" of biblical verses, and God would then enlighten his understanding to include philosophy and Kabbalah as well.

But as much as philosophers have delved into knowledge and religion, they have not discovered the essence of the holy names which the Kabbalists understood. Yet even the words of the latter must be tempered with philosophical logic and historical knowledge; the person who has no knowledge of either encounters a stumbling block and will not know in what way he has failed. Therefore, not only a person who has not delved fully into the entire Talmud and *halakhic* interpretations, and the arbiters, cannot deal with esoteric meanings, it is also demanded that the student orient his thinking with true philosophical logic as well as acquiring historical knowledge and sensitivity so that he may give everything its historical basis; then he will be discerning.[4]

In other words, a biblical verse could not be interpreted by detaching it from its real historical context, nor could one understand the true depth of the Bible except on the basis of historical study because the Divine word which was revealed in prophecy was a historical fact. It was directed toward a certain historical reality to which the Bible testified and it was correctly interpreted only through knowledge of that reality. Again, Hirschensohn did not, by this, dismiss the philosophical or Kabbalistic interpretation but said that that interpretation did not displace the simple historical meaning. Rather, it was built on that historical meaning.

The issue of historical research, therefore, was not external to the world of traditional interpretation. It was an essential need of that interpretation, and for that reason not only apologetic motives necessitated an objective grappling with biblical criticism. If the Bible was not seen as a consistent historical tract from the point of view of chronological continuity, as well as in consonance with various historical testimonies about those same events, even the essential basis for a valid homiletic understanding would be lost. This, of course, led first to the effort to solve the great difficulties found in the biblical chronology, and subsequently to the task of solving the problems which stemmed from the seeming contradictions between biblical testimonies. Hirschensohn's scientific solution was based on the assumption that "there is no concept of 'early' or 'late' in the Torah," the bold significance of which was that the sequence in which the texts were presented was not necessarily the order in which the events about which they testified happened or in which laws were told to Moses. Therefore, if the original order of narrative and revelation was discovered, all the difficulties would disappear and a brilliantly coherent historical testimony would become evident.

In *Yamim M'Kedem*, Hirschensohn used this assumption to resolve contradictions in the biblical chronology, while in *Seder La-Mikrah*, he proposed a detailed text criticism, i.e., a succession of the biblical chapters which was different than the existing version; in this way he thought to dispel everything that seemed to be, according to the existing version, a contradiction which placed doubt on the Divine origin of the Torah and the authenticity of its historical testimony. Thus Hirschensohn gave biblical criticism its true place. No scientific consideration could undermine faith in the prophecy of Moses, but belief alone could not paper-over certain occurrences or seeming inconsistencies in the biblical version. Until these difficulties were settled, there would not be a solid foundation for theological interpretation.

Hirschensohn's theory was that Moses received the entire Torah through prophecy, but that the words were spoken to him, and the scrolls written down by him, at different times; that he did not connect the separate scrolls according to the order in which they were said and written but joined them together in a different sequence, and, at times, even juxtaposed sections and sentences so that earlier ones were set in later while later ones were placed first. These transitions could not be felt through a rapid reading because the new fusion was done with great skill. The difficulties, therefore, did not appear to the average student, but a close reading by Sages and men of science revealed the artificial seams, either by exposing the extension of a subject which had ended abruptly in another place, or by contradictions, duplications and gaps. If this was understood, one could, with great effort, deduce the original order in which the words were said to Moses by God.

Hirschensohn believed this to be the viewpoint of Rabbi Ishmael and his school of thought, and the root of the controversy between him and Rabbi Akiva. Hirschensohn also thought that "the Mystery of the

Creation" and "the Mystery of the Chariot" in the writings of the Sages were directly connected to the issue of the sequence of the scrolls, and the interpreters of these phrases were mistaken if they gave philosophical or Kabbalistic readings to them. The homiletic key in this matter was also historical — "the Mystery of Creation" was the esoteric original order of composition of the verses and chapters of the creation narrative, and the "Mystery of the Chariot" was the esoteric original order of the chapters of the vision of the chariot. When one knew these esoteric orders, one could then penetrate the depths of the literal reading of the two stories.

It was not difficult to understand why the Sages had kept the knowledge of the correct sequence of the Scriptures a secret since it could have aroused confusion and doubt among the people. But why did Moses confuse the order of the chapters? Hirschensohn's answer was surprising: "He jumbled them purposefully in order to hint at laws and interpretations, morals, and also secrets of the Torah which I clarified in the book, *Moreh L'Morim Nevukhim (A Guide to Perplexed Teachers)*, in various places."[5] In other words, the historical connection was made through a conscious and well-deliberated change in the sequence of the scrolls and chapters. This had to be understood when one began with the literal meaning so that in it and deriving from it, one would understand the homiletic interpretation as well. The homiletic interpretation, arrived at according to the methods set forth in the Oral Law, did not violate the biblical writings, even when it strayed greatly from the literal meaning, because the Torah which was interpreted according to the literal meaning latent within it in accordance with the original composition, could also be interpreted correctly according to the subsequent composition through the homiletic meaning.

The Torah held within it these two methods as two equally authentic means for understanding the great significances to which it alluded. Moreover, a dimension of secrecy was created in the revealed literal meaning as well as a dimension of simple revelation in the homiletic meaning which disclosed esoteric meanings. The homiletic meaning deciphered the connection which was revealed, and the literal meaning was deciphered historically through a covert connection. The two interpretive methods and the two dimensions of significance — the literal-historical, on the one hand, and the theological or homiletic-ethical, on the other — met in the text itself, in the two modalities of their compilation. Hirschensohn accepted as historical fact — given, absolute proof — that the rules of homiletic interpretation of the Oral Law, both in *halakhah* and *aggadah,* or "the methods by which the Torah is studied," were divinely revealed to Moses, and that the use of these methods were to be found in the written Torah itself. His position was that these were not logical rules, identical to the rules of Aristotelian logic; these were interpretive rules based on the authority of prophetic revelation and tradition, to discover what the Torah had hidden in the secret of its special sequence.

This solution was still not satisfactory, either from the scientific or Torah perspective. As two different perceptions which required completely different methods of reading, there was something arbitrary and forced in a purely technical separation between an understanding of the literal text and an understanding of the homiletic meaning. Was there no objective, essential relationship between the interpretation that stemmed from research into the literal meaning, and the meaning that stemmed from the homiletic interpretation? Did not the historical, ethical, and theological truths need each other and directly nourish each other? Hirschensohn's answer was positive. He based it on a scientific analysis of the homiletic method, and on an analysis of the essential connection between it and the literal meaning, on the one hand, and the totality of the social and historical experience of generations of Jewish interpreters, on the other.

And here, as well, is the method on which I built my work, *Naim Zmirot (The Pleasant Singer),* about the Book of Psalms, in order to interpret the Bible according to the "literal meaning of the homily," based on the interpretations of the Sages, even if they did not refer to the literal meaning but only to that part of the Torah which is termed "homiletics." The meaning cannot exceed what is inherent in the literal text, but all of the constructs on which the interpreters founded their academies whose pillars were made of silver, encased in gold, hung with royal purple to beautify and exalt the idea by the animated spirit of their homiletic methodology — were an unbroken, simple literal meaning. This means that every interpreter was faced with a certain literal meaning of the Bible which was used as a basis on which to build the homiletic interpretation, and it is this specific literal meaning which I seek in my book, in interpreting the Psalms.

This is because the Psalms, as well as all the other poetic books which express poetic meanings, cannot be rendered in one absolute literal meaning, which we may state as the only true meaning of the verse. Indeed, the words of the Torah are as a hammer that breaks a rock, in which not only the deeper meaning but also the literal meaning can be interpreted in several ways. Just as the interest of *halakhic* Torah scholars is to discover the intent of the Sages in their interpretation of commandments and *halakhah*, so the same is true for the *aggadah* and the Scripture interpretation. Even if we refrain from entering into the area of deeper meanings (of Pardes: *p'shat, remez, drosh, sod*), and search for the literal meaning only, even then we must determine which literal meaning the Sages had before them as they studied a text, and since we do not have an extant version of their literal interpretation because all that we have from their writings is in the realm of Pardes, we must seek the underlying literal bases upon which they built their homiletics. They knew that the Bible cannot exceed its literal sense, therefore they built their homilies on a certain literal foundation, and then they developed it to increase wisdom. Truly, the edifice they constructed — upon the literal meaning — with the stones of homiletic interpretations are great structures whose lofty towers stretch to the heavens of symbolic, homiletic and esoteric meanings.[6]

Indeed, the rendering of the "literal meaning of the homily" was mainly a homiletic interpretation of poetic writings which had an ambiguous literal meaning. However, in the book *Nimukei Rashi* and in other essays, Hirschensohn made a wider use of this principle so as to demonstrate that the Oral Law always related literally to the written Torah, even when expressing the direct thinking of every sage in his own time and place. These were not separate dimensions of understanding grafted onto each other through technical and arbitrary means. There was one truth, a living truth, which was revealed in different facets in two interpretive dimensions and, in fact, the scientific philological study of the methods of the Oral Law in its affinity to the written Torah can demonstrate this.

There was an instructive parallelism between Hirschensohn's approach and the Rambam's approach to biblical interpretation; the similarity to the Rambam was made explicit in the section quoted above on Moses' intent in changing the biblical sequence. The Rambam

126

also assumed the principle of "there is no concept of 'early' and 'late' in the Bible" as the basis for his interpretations; he believed that there was a deliberate purpose to the intermingled sequence in the Bible, i.e., the intent to conceal the internal significance of the Torah from the unworthy person and to hint at it to whoever was worthy. And he also searched for an exact method by which to interpret the secret of the Torah through understanding the various aspects of the simple literal sense. The difference between Hirschensohn and the Rambam could be seen in the modalities and explanations of how the biblical sections should be merged but, given the passage of time, even this difference was a result of the same goal: to reconcile what was accepted as the truth of the Torah and what was regarded as scientific truth, and to reach a genuine synthesis of scientific interpretation with traditional interpretation, in such a way that each would not only dwell with the other without quarrel or mutual invalidation, but would reinforce the interpretations of the other, within its own system. Consequently, scientific study would confirm the validity of the homiletic method for the biblical text to which it was directed, just as the homiletic method needed scientific research to arrive at the literal meaning, and to define the "literal meaning" of the homily. Finally, like the Rambam, Hirschensohn also applied his assumptions to detailed interpretations whose value lay in their depth and originality, even if the reader was unprepared to accept his interpretive methodology as scientific.

Notes

1. *Malki BaKodesh*, Section Two, Response to Question 6.
2. See *Yamim M'Kedem, HeHahronologia HaBiblit*, Jerusalem, 1908; *Seder LaMikrah*, or *Mukdam V'Meuhar B'Meorah*, Jerusalem, 1933.
3. *Eileh Divrei HaBrit*, Part Three, p. 22.
4. *Ibid.*, Part One, p. 138.
5. *Sefer Nimukei Rashi*, p. 26, S2.
6. *Ibid.*, p. 25, S1.

Chapter 10

A CRITIQUE OF "FALSE CONCEPTS AND TRUTH"

It is evident from the material presented in previous chapters that Hirschensohn preferred considering issues that pertained to practical life. An exemplary *halakhic* expert, he made his principles clear as he confronted problems which arose within the social reality; and in relating to problems at the highest theoretical level, he also proposed principles for practical solutions. Thus even when called upon to formulate the principles of his *weltanschauung*, Hirschensohn frequently emphasized his assumption that the development of a world view should not be sought for its own sake, but was needed to guide one's deeds. He stressed the premise that Judaism was always directed toward practice, and that conceptual analysis, for its own sake, was never held in esteem. The paramount question was: to what extent, and how, to act? Conceptual analysis was necessary as long as it was a condition for obtaining a lucid answer to this question. But this preference for the practical did not lead to any disregard to provide a systematic underpinning for basic assumptions. Though Hirschensohn did not have the same degree of originality in the theological area as he did in the area of *halakhic* thought, he did have his own thesis, and within the context of his works there is much of interest in it.

Hirschensohn's philosophical book, *Musagei Shav V'HaEmet (Concepts of Falsehood and Truth),*[1] was written over a long period of time. In fact, the writing was done without a preplanned program, by the compilation of segments of work, throughout almost the entire period of his literary activity; thus it reflected the consistent organic process of his spiritual development. Even when it was completed, it appears that Hirschensohn did not impose any systematic structure on the work. A collection of short essays, written as opportunity allowed, it contained ideas that arose during his lifetime, or comments on books that he studied closely (i.e., Rambam's *Guide of the Perplexed* and Spinoza's *Ethics*) which he considered to be of major consequence. This method of writing faithfully mirrored Hirschensohn's approach to the realm of spiritual creativity; accordingly, it can be presented as systematic.

Consistent with his practical approach, he did not attribute any importance to abstract overall theory. For Hirschensohn, philosophy was mainly a conceptual critique; it was a critique of the assumptions that served the individual in his thinking about the issues of life which required that he react to them directly. In this sense, there was no one who did not have his own "philosophy," even if he had not bothered to formulate it; the philosopher was someone who had freed himself from holding on to mistakes in his reactions, or the reactions of the community, in order to examine the assumptions underlying the accepted behavior in his surroundings and thus influence their rectification. According to Hirschensohn, philosophy was an independent judgment of one's common sense about the assumptions and conceptual understandings which guide people's behavior in all aspects of their lives. And in this context, it did not require an *a priori* overall approach. On the contrary, its strength was revealed precisely in considering specific, individual issues in order to illuminate them thoroughly. Nonetheless, the accumulation of conclusions which arose from discussions of many separate issues such as these, resulted in a total view that was unified by its critical approach.

In this respect, Hirschensohn was very different from the models of philosophical thought which he himself presented as sources of influence: the Kabbalah, the Rambam and Spinoza. One could say that this was precisely a reflection of his openness to the influence of modern philosophy, and especially the influence of American pragmatism. Nonetheless, there is a parallelism between this method of writing and the Rambam's method, and there is also a conscious parallelism between this method of theoretical writing and the random method in which a *halakhic* theoretician writes about the various issues of life.

It was in this way that Hirschensohn gave a very broad interpretation to the Rambam's method of thinking in the first part of *Guide of the Perplexed* which culminated in the theory of "negative attributes," i.e., a critical examination of the accepted views that led to the recognition of truth by rejecting that which was false or mistaken in regular, conventional, uncritical thought. Hirschensohn's manner of choosing topics for deliberation was also not systematic, in contradistinction to the Rambam's; rather, it was open to a full range of topics in keeping with the practice of a *halakhic* theoretician who responds to each current topic that presents itself in daily life. But the accumulated result was that Hirschensohn at last arrived at a theology of his own which could be systematically reformulated.

Moreover, despite the many differences between him and the Rambam — who maintained a crystallized philosophical method — one must consider Hirschensohn a disciple of the Rambam in this area as well; albeit, a disciple who had already engaged in a detailed study of other influences and had returned to his first master while still not relinquishing the stamp of studies contrary in theory to those of the Rambam.

Schematically, the development of Hirschensohn's philosophical theory can be described according to the following stages: first, the study of Kabbalistic literature which had a great influence on the prevailing mood of his surroundings when he was young. Next, reservations about the Kabbalah and a growing conviction as to the Rambam's method. This was followed by a grappling with the challenge of Spinoza, and, in the face of this challenge, a renewed affirmation of the Rambam's approach. These were the formative influences consciously reflected throughout Hirschensohn's work. But, as noted earlier, study reveals both the impact of Rabbi Nahman Krochmal's *Guide of the Perplexed of the Time*, and of American pragmatism which he used as well to critically interpret the Rambam's theories. A summary, therefore, of what Hirschensohn accepted or rejected at each of the stages noted above would be worthwhile at this point.

Initially, Hirschensohn was influenced by the Kabbalah[2] which was held in respect in his circles. He soon felt, however, that it ran counter to his general approach and an ambivalent assessment can be discerned in his book, *Sefer Musagei Shav V'HaEmet (Concepts of Truth and Falsehood)*. Hirschensohn saw the Kabbalah as the result of a later development of an ancient Jewish tradition in which the influences of Plato's and Plotinus's philosophies were incorporated into a matrix of original Jewish thought which relied on the symbolism of lights. Like Rabbi Nahman Krochmal, Hirschensohn valued the tradition on which the Kabbalah was based as a positive traditional study, but he felt that subsequently it had been corrupted, the main distortion being unrealistic thought which led to the embodiment of abstract concepts until they actually became objects. In other words, a conceptual system of human thought about God as He related to the world as its Creator and Guiding Light was turned by the Kabbalists

131

into a network of objects which would gradually, by means of the theory of emanation, bridge the gap between man and God. Thus man was bound through a system of essences which emanated, as it were, from God Himself, and thus man was presented with the possibility of being an active part of the Divine power which shaped him and his world. There were many concepts of truth in the Kabbalah, but its misguided understanding of the theory of emanation introduced a most dangerous error into its truth. One had to retrace one's course and set the perspective of human thought so that it did not overstep the boundaries of man's distinct essence which had to be manifest in his thought about his Creator, as well.[3]

Hirschensohn's attitude toward Spinoza was more complex. *Ab initio*, he was faced with the *halakhic* issue. How should he relate to the man behind the theory, and how should he relate to a theory which had been so closely identified, from the very beginning, with extreme apostasy? In this respect, his attitude toward Spinoza and toward Spinoza's theory was a reflection of Hirschensohn's basic attitude toward modern culture. Spinoza embodied the challenge, at once enticing and frightening, of a crossover beyond the boundary of Judaism. There was a psychological issue here that was no less important than the intellectual one. Hirschensohn discovered Spinoza with the same sense of surprise as one would have at learning about something which at first seems incomprehensible and even threatening. It became comprehensible and quite clear, as well as non-threatening. When it became non-threatening, Hirschensohn lost interest and the attraction Spinoza's philosophy held was dissipated through a critical penetration to the "secret" which was hidden, as it were, beyond the seductive wall of foreignness. If one only dared lift the veil, a familiar world would be found which could be related to with critical tolerance. In this way, the process continued.

Hirschensohn had been influenced by the magic of Spinoza through several brilliant lectures on his theories which he heard while in Constantinople. He delved critically into the *Ethics* and then, for an unexplained reason, stopped in the middle of a passage. At some point his interest flagged once he discovered the essence of Spinoza's thought and found the source of his error. From then on, he appeared to feel, he would find nothing new or edifying.[4] The experience apparently explains his *halakhic* position toward Spinoza — the man, and his work — which was that one should not consider him an apostate. He did indeed err and the error was grave, but since he erred guilelessly and maintained what he thought to be the absolute truth, it was impossible to condemn him for his error. Except for a deed contrary to *halakhah*, one was not judged; even if the views ran counter to the Torah, one was not judged for beliefs which he held because those were thoughts. Moreover, Hirschensohn saw that Spinoza's psyche possessed a very strong religious tendency; because he recognized that the comprehensive and unifying reality of the world was God, he repeatedly sought to equate all the characteristics of God with his concept of a transcendental God. In other words, Spinoza's misguided attitude toward the concept of God was nonetheless a proper religious attitude of a man toward his God. In Hirschensohn's opinion this meant that from a *halakhic* viewpoint Spinoza stayed within the tolerable boundaries of the Torah, and one should relate to his theory through a confrontation with the issues, for his error was neither accidental nor insincere. From this point of view, it would appear that Spinoza was no more inappropriate than was the Kabbalah, and in retrospect, the confrontation with Spinoza represented a more important formative stage than that of the Kabbalah in crystallizing Hirschensohn's theory.

Where, then, did Spinoza err? He erred in that he thought of the unity of the cosmos — which is indeed the Ultimate Substance that the human mind can conceive of in positive terms — as God, i.e., as being *causa sua*. In Hirschensohn's opinion, the error was expressed in the term "*causa sua*," as distinguished from the term, "necessary existence," by which God should really be described. Spinoza knew, according to this explanation, that the General Substance, the unity of all the substances of which the world is constituted, is still not a necessary existent. One must assume a cause which generated it and everything contained within it, but since human reason cannot conceive of any entity beyond the General Substance of the world, and since Spinoza rejected any assumption of an entity beyond human thought as unworthy of thinking, he could not escape an internal contradiction: the ultimately caused substance became, for him, its own cause. Hirschensohn believed that to be a clear error, since the concept of causality necessitates the transcendence of the cause to its effect. There is nothing which is a cause unto itself. There is only the necessary existent which is in and of itself transcendental to human thought since man is a created being.

Of course, in such an internally consistent theory as Spinoza's, this lone error was constantly built upon throughout his entire system.

A blurring of the distinction between the cause and the effect of the Ultimate Substance which includes all substances resulted in the blurring of the distinction between the Ultimate Substance (God) and its constituent substances. For Spinoza, the Ultimate Substance was the one unique entity, and everything which appears as its components or parts are none other than its modalities.

Moreover, the blurring of the distinction between the Ultimate Substance and its components also led to a blurring of the distinction between material forms and spiritual forms. These were replaced by the concept of expansion and thought as two modalities of an infinity of attributes of the sole Ultimate Substance. This string of errors stemmed from a primary mistake: the assumption that the cause could be immanent in its effect, i.e., identical to it. An identity between cause and effect would require that everything be identical.

The discovery of this basic error at once undermined the entire system. Hirschensohn thus returned to the Rambam's concept. It assumed that beyond the kabbalistic theory which regarded the world as a continuous effluence derived from God, and beyond Spinoza's theory which identified the world with God, God is the Necessary Existent. He created the world which is composed of many substances which are external to Him. God related to the world as Creator, and the world related to God as His creation. In this sense there was a positive concept of God, but only in this respect. The essence of God is transcendental to human thought, just as it is transcendental to the world. When man learns about the world he draws closer to God as its Creator, but he can never conceive of Him.[5]

Since Hirschensohn affirmed the distinction between cause and effect, he also affirmed the concept of the world as a unity of many parts, as well as the distinction between material and spiritual entities. But at this point one can see the innovative deviation from the Rambam's Aristotelian conceptual system. Hirschensohn did not need the concepts of "form" and "matter" which are characteristic of Aristotelian physics. In their stead he introduced the distinction between substances which "have dimensions" and can be perceived through one's senses, and substances which "are measureless" or spiritual substances which are perceived to exist whether through man's consciousness of himself as possessor of a soul, or through the presence of movement which has no immanent cause in entities "having dimensions."[6]

This distinction derived from the primary conclusion that the cause was transcendental to the effect, and just as this necessitated a total, super-worldly cause for the entire world, so it necessitated a particular cause for the unique movement of each individual form, insofar as it was not a mechanical movement caused by being touched by another entity "having form." Hirschensohn did not try to explain the action of the spiritual entities on the entities "with form." He posited it as a scientific fact to which nature testified in all its segments. Indeed, it would appear that there is a clear transfer of the "correlative" relation between God as the Necessary Existent which is the cause of everything, and the world as a general effect, to the area of the relationships between parts of the world and the forces propelling them; a clear concept that there is a "correlation" between these forces and the substantial entities. This is the assumption which necessarily derives from the multiplicity of individual actions which we cannot explain by one cause, and from the essence of the dimensional substances, although the manner in which the spiritual and the material affect each other cannot be conceptualized.

In any case, Hirschensohn's conception was hierarchical. The whole world is composed of a great quantity of parts, joined to each other. They become entities which contain two orders: one of dimensional and one of spiritual substances. This double hierarchy is most complex in man. This is because besides the coordination between the functions of the various limbs, a phenomenon which testified to the existence of a spiritual force supervising it, man had the consciousness of an ego or "soul." The soul was the highest spiritual entity within the hierarchy of spiritual and material forces which comprised man. Each one of the limbs of the body was a composition of entities with dimensions, and a hierarchy of spiritual forces which activated them. The ego was the highest spiritual entity which was connected to all the other entities which activated the body's limbs, and as such it influenced the direction of the activity of the body as a whole, but did not directly control the action of all the parts. It supervised them and led them in a general way. Its control was limited, but this disadvantage was also an advantage. The ego of man was not directed at the activity of the body alone. It could also be directed at itself, as the focus of separate activity. It could as well be directed toward a spiritual reality above it.[7]

In the critical approach of *Sefer Musagei Shav V'HaEmet*, Hirschensohn rejected concepts in the theories of other philosophers without necessarily presenting a full unfolding of his own solutions. This was, in fact, the shortcoming of the book. The ideas noted above were not adequately developed; they remained only as general assumptions. Hirschensohn's ideas were elaborated in a limited measure only, solely in the direction which was of most interest to him, the theological direction. This was especially true of the theory of the ego noted above which, in fact, Hirschensohn had recourse to in order to provide a scientific-philosophical explication to the phenomenon of prophecy.

What is prophecy? Hirschensohn's reply was similar to that of the Rambam in that it upheld the psychological explanation that prophecy was a supreme state of human consciousness. But the quality of Hirschensohn's explanation was different. An examination of his claims discloses that they contained inchoate elements of modern depth psychology alongside certain influences of Rabbi Yehuda Halevi's concept of prophecy. The ego of man was directed toward the body and its actions. Normally, it was not directed toward itself, but acted externally. Nonetheless, with some effort the ego was capable of observing itself during its actions. This is also a regular voluntary matter, but in this state the ego did not recognize itself as distinct from the body as it presided over the actions of its limbs and directed them. Through normal reflex action, the soul was conscious of itself in its connection to the body which was the ego of the body. It was an unusual occurrence when the ego conceived of itself as entirely detached, beyond its connection to the body. While awake, this was not at all possible because the waking state was a state of alertness toward external surroundings. But during sleep, when the responsibility of the soul toward the body was partially tempered, it could happen that the soul might confront itself in a dream, without connection to the body and with no consciousness of its connection to the body. This was not a usual occurrence but it was one that was experienced by all individuals at some time. In a dream it was possible for an individual to envision himself as if in an experience external to himself, as an "other" whom he knew intimately. This was still not prophecy, but it was an experience preparatory to prophecy. To go one step further, the release from the connection for activating the body allowed the soul to be receptive to other spiritual manifestations, equal to it and even more sublime. Other spiritual entities appeared then to the soul. It related to them and experienced their presence and, at the moment that the ego observed itself as it reflected spiritual experiences beyond itself through the ego (which was distinct from it), it conceived the spiritual entity above it, and this experience was prophecy.[8]

There were, then, spiritual entities beyond the ego of man. These entities were more encompassing than man, and were closer to the concept of the totality of creation, a concept which made the relationship of God to His world unique. The prophet gained with the same supreme conception in his prophecy, but, according to Hirschensohn, this was not a purely intellectual achievement but a presence comparable to the experience of a presence of which Halevi spoke. Yet, again the affinity with the Rambam reappeared, and could be seen in the emphasis on the intentional human effort in prophecy, and in addition, in the emphasis on the role of human consciousness in shaping the images and concepts of the prophet. Moreover, Hirschensohn developed the Rambam's approach in the direction of psychological individualism. God's revelation is identified as a constant presence in creation. It was man who was receptive to meet God, and that which man grasped about God was conditional on his individual ability. Every prophet had his own grasp of the Divine. According to the Rambam, the differences were mainly differences of degree in which individuality was not discerned except in the number of one's spiritual limitations, while Hirschensohn perceived of the soul, in its positive uniqueness, as having an active role in prophecy. The prophet conceived of the Divine presence through the fullness of his individual soul which he envisioned as external to himself. The significance of this was that the personality of man, his unique spirituality, was that which perceived the Divine presence; the prophet's concept of God thus took on the complete unique and unequivocal nature of the prophet's personality. Prophecy therefore became a clearly personal experience, without denying its objective, authoritative validity.

These statements were charged with great significance, beyond the concept of prophecy as a concept of the religious experience in the pattern of Divine worship in daily life, because what was valid for prophecy, as the supreme form of religious experience, could also hold for ritual, especially for prayer. Ritual was the symbolic practice through which man expressed his desire to draw closer to his God.[9] This, of course, was man's need, not God's need. Hirschensohn therefore rejected the Kabbalistic approach in explaining the reasons for the commandments and basically accepted, even in many of the details, the Rambam's approach which presented the commandments that related to ritual as an educational system. It was not surprising that among the ritualistic commandments Hirschensohn ascribed the greatest importance to prayer as distinct from the sacrifices. This was already evident in his controversy with Rabbi Kook on the issue of renewing the sacrificial service in the Temple. But his comments on prayer appeared to reflect the same development of the Rambam's views in an individualistic-psychological direction. In prayer, man was alone with his soul, striving to be his own judge. If he succeeded, he would attain an experience parallel to that of the prophet, a kind of observation of his soul as a distinct being and through it of the Divine presence reflected in it. In other words, through prayer man could also experience the presence of his Creator through his soul; this was the individualism which could be seen not only through the limitations of personal ability but also in the awakening and illumination of all the positive characteristics of the individual soul. Man experienced his essentiality to the full, in the presence of his Creator. Once again, it should not be surprising that Hirschensohn did not accept the preference that was characteristic of the Rambam, of pure intellectual activity, neither in prophecy nor in prayer. The emotional and recollective elements were no less important, in his opinion, than the intellectual elements. Prayer was a lyric and a melody; it was memory and remembrance before God; it was the personal meeting of man with his Creator. But it was the personal movement of the individual which aroused all the forces of his soul in meeting his Creator which made it possible for him to be worthy of a meeting of this nature. God was equally available to all, and each individual explained in his own special way the Divine presence in his soul.

The inclination toward psychological individualism resembled the inclination toward historical relativity discussed above. Together they constituted the basis for a far-reaching, tolerant approach to the different trends within Judaism, and also to other religions and world views external to it. But a correct understanding of Hirschensohn's works requires one to stress that psychological individualism, as well as the recognition of the development of historical relativity, was limited by belief in the absolutely imperative, "objective" Divine revelation. Personal experience revealed the affirmative action of the soul in its connection to the true God, the infinite revelation of Whom was one and eternal; history was a result of limited human endeavor, but God had determined its destiny, and at Mount Sinai the Jewish people were granted the revelation of the Torah and commandments whose imperative validity was eternal. In fact, internal tolerance had limits as well. Beyond them it was perhaps possible to maintain a permissive understanding of the possibility of human error rooted in the life of the soul or in the historical process, but in no way could Hirschensohn agree, or recognize the possibility, that an opinion which deviated from these limits would be valid.

Hirschensohn asserted several times that "religion" — if by this term one understood that which European languages connoted as "religia" — was a decidedly personal, intimate matter. Each individual had his unique religiosity, both as to the nature of the spiritual experience which he achieved in prayer or in his intuitive cognition of the world around him, as well as from the image or concept which God represented within his soul.[10] One neither could nor should legislate about faith in this connection. In its essence it was the exclusive domain of the individual, and in fact man stood before God as an individual. It was as an individual man came to know Him, and there was no greater distortion than dogmatic coercion in this area. Judaism, claimed Hirschensohn — and a fairly long tradition of Jewish thinkers in ancient times as well as the modern era supported his claim — had no dogmatic coercion of faith in this connection, and this was its clear advantage over dogmatic Christianity.[11] It was easy to prove that this assertion opened the door wide to a multiplicity of ways of thinking which sought to advance man toward knowing his Creator. There was no one true theology because there was no infinite theology which could encompass the possible infinities of the perceptions of individuals, while real content was found only in the conceptions of these individuals. Nonetheless, Judaism did fix a clear framework, and it appeared that this framework was clear not only on the issue of practical behavior, but also on the issue of faith. If "religion" as such was left to the individual, then ethics — said Hirschensohn — were left to the individual in the public sphere. Ethics were by their nature normative, and Judaism as a normative ethic fixed clear limits for the individual which was as it should be. Indeed, it determined its limits through religion, i.e., through the authority of Divine revelation, and it could be seen that its normativeness was not only in the area of ethics but in the area of prayer and even in the area of faith. However unique the individual perception of each Jew might be, it had imperative limits. It posited that God was only Creator of the world and its Leader; He made the covenant with His people and gave them the Torah. The individual who rejected the first part of this credo placed himself outside Judaism with respect to "religion"; the individual who rejected the second part removed himself from Judaism by abrogating the covenant of the people.

In following Hirschensohn's deliberations on this issue, one sees a seemingly internal contradiction which could not be reconciled: individualism and historical relativity, on the one hand, and the determination of objective religious truth, on the other; far-reaching tolerance, on the one hand, and unequivocal rejection of paganism and Christianity, on the other. Indeed, Hirschensohn displayed his broad-mindedness even toward Christianity. He could understand the causes of its error, but sufferance for error was not to be taken as tolerance for a multitude of opinions, i.e., on the assumption that these wrong opinions could also contain a germ of truth. It must be admitted that Hirschensohn's statements on these issues were actually far from clear and unequivocal. The ambivalence was clearly felt, but it would be unjustified to describe them in terms of inconsistency or contradiction. The issue could be delineated properly if the area of the individual relationship of man to his God was determined as an area of the self-action of the positive forces of the soul — emotion, imagination, thought — toward an *objective reality,* which man had to accept as a given and had to obey. Each individual could, of course, create his own idea of the truth which God revealed in His Creation and His word, but he was subject to the objective validity of the revelation itself. The individual was sovereign in using the powers given him. He was not sovereign in conceiving the reality itself. If he knew this, if he recognized that he was a created being whom God led and commanded, then he recognized the crucial objective basis of every subjective relationship. If he erred and considered his subjective attitude an absolute determination of "his" truth, then he had already entered the area of pagan falsehood; in other words, recognition of the universal basis of the Jewish faith: one God Who created the world and led it. This was the basis for all true individuality; tolerance that went beyond this limit waived any criterion of truth and equated the relative with the false and imaginary. A Jew was therefore obligated as a human being, and as a member of the Jewish people in particular, to an objective truth which was revealed in his history.

With these lines the issue comes full circle. The process of "drawing close" to modernity which was found in Hirschensohn's theory in the area of national, social and political ideology, can also be seen in the area of theological ideology. There, Hirschensohn drew close to the edge of the possible limit of liberal and democratic ideas but did not blur the distinction between a democracy rooted in the idea of the sovereignty of man, and a democracy rooted in the idea of man's being commanded by his Creator. Here, Hirschensohn came close to the possible limit of the notions of individualism, historical relativity and tolerance which characterized modern culture, but he did not blur the distinction between individualism and tolerance rooted in the idea of the sovereignty of human thought in the area of faith and ethics, and the individualism and tolerance rooted in faith in the One and Absolute God Who created the world and directed it. Hirschensohn's great achievement, in both areas, was in a clear presentation of the tension between the areas, and in his daring to fix the boundaries of truth of each one of them, in order to reach a solution which could guide a new national-religious creativity.

Notes

1. Jerusalem, 1932.
2. He himself testified to this. See the biographical remark in his book, *Sefer Musagei Shav V'HaEmet*, Ch. 4, "Spirituality."
3. See, for example: *ibid.*, Ch. 14. Also, Ch. 40, "Emanation, Ten Spheres, Spirit."
4. *Ibid.*, end of Section Three, p. 120.
5. This conclusion is repeated time and again in the book, especially in the remarks about Spinoza's *Ethics*, pp. 73-74, as well as in the body of the book. See, for example, Ch. 27.
6. This distinction is presented in Ch. 3, "Abstraction and Form," and is repeated many times. On the connection between "substances having form" and "substances which are measureless," see Ch. 20.
7. See Ch. 39, "Soul and Spirit, the 'Ego,' Humanity and Man."
8. See Ch. 3, as well as Ch. 52.
9. See Ch. 50, as well as Ch. 53.
10. See, for example, Ch. 54.
11. See *ibid.*, the end of the chapter.

Chapter 11

THE THEORIES OF RABBI HIRSCHENSOHN AND RABBI KOOK

Parallels and contrasts between the theories of Rabbi Hirschensohn and Rabbi Kook[1] were noted at the beginning of this monograph; both schools of thought had historical antecedents. Rabbi Kook's theories advanced the ideas of Rabbi Yehuda Halevi and the Kabbalists, while the theories of Rabbi Hirschensohn furthered the ideas of the Rambam and his followers. Both men confronted the reality of the modern era which is clearly seen by the way in which they developed the ideas of their predecessors. A comparison of their theories, however, reveals a typological distinction: a theory which posited as its center the experience of the residence of God in the midst of His people and His land, versus a theory which posited as its center behavior according to God's ways, that is, seeking truth and doing good; a theory attentive to the inner flow of the Jewish people's history and the history of revelation in the people's destiny, life and creativity and defines Judaism as the essence of the totality of human culture, versus a theory attentive to the general continuity of human history and cultural creativity which sees the history of the Jewish people as only a part of human culture; and finally, a theory which conceives of the Jewish people and all its existential attributes of history, land, language and literature as a supranatural emanation which strives toward the end of redemption conceived of as a supernatural wholeness, versus a theory which conceives of the Jewish people and all of its existential attributes as a natural development, and strives toward the end of redemption conceived of as perfection in terms of ethical-social and religious achievements limited within the boundaries of human nature. These are two approaches that developed throughout the history of Jewish thought for which support can be found in the Sources, both in the biblical literature and in the ancient literature of the Oral Law. There were periods when one was more dominant and periods when the other dominated, but it would appear that a new interpretation of one always served to stimulate a parallel development within the second, countering it in a critical and complementary tension.

The religious ideology which evolved within the national-Zionist movement in Eastern Europe and in Eretz Israel initially supported the course of thought typical of Rabbi Yehuda Halevi and the Kabbalists. This ideology allowed them to contend with the extensive changes in the internal and external life of the Jewish people without denying the positive aspects of the changes, and without creating a split in the continuity of a Torah-directed lifestyle and thought. By recourse to the ideational tools of Rabbi Yehuda Halevi and the Kabbalists, it was possible to reflect the new changes within the internal fullness of tradition, and to regard the external influences as though they were derived from inner sources. Rabbi Kook was the outstanding proponent of this approach. But it quickly became clear that the drawback of this approach was that it related positively to new cultural developments from the outside without being familiar with their proper historical context or their full significance within that context. Thus a different systematic concept was needed which employed methods derived from the Rambam's school of thought. Rabbi Hirschensohn was the most prominent and consistent representative of this trend.

Rabbi Kook and Rabbi Hirschensohn were very much alike in their positive reactions to the realities of the modern era. Within each of them there pulsated the aspiration to restore to the Jews the full life of a people: i.e., a people that lived in its own land, in a majority society of its own, in its own state, as did all the nations around it. In each of them there pulsated the aspiration to overcome a constriction in cultural creativity which had necessarily been caused by life in Exile. Their concern was not for "religion" in its restricted meaning — as a system of commandments, especially those between man and his Creator — but for a comprehensive teaching for life which unfolded with the expansion of societal creativity in economics, politics, science, art and higher thought. The young generation of Jews was attracted to the growth of such ideas among the European nations. Therefore, access to such creativity — no less inferior in level or scope, perhaps higher — had to be allowed to them within the context of their own people.

In both Rabbi Kook and Rabbi Hirschensohn there was a strong aspiration for the independence of the Jewish people, for leaving the narrow straits of Exile, and for a redemption that would signal a comprehensive change in the life of the people. For both of them Zionism was a renaissance in this all-encompassing sense, and each of them understood the far-reaching nature of the change it meant in the lifestyle of the Jewish people and its relationship to the external world. This was the basis of the enormous audacity that character-ized their attitude to the Torah-traditional foundation of their thought. Nonetheless, notwithstanding the similarity between them, their efforts took them in opposite directions, and the result was a sharp confrontation.

Rabbi Kook's views were based on the assumption that the Jewish people were the core of humankind and as such embodied in its essence and in its internality everything that was positive in humanity, both potentially and actually. Young Jews who rejected the Torah and its commandments and who were attracted to the great achievements of Western culture thought these achievements to be essentially external to a Judaism that seemed to them impoverished and insular. In fact, their enthusiastic attraction was in itself proof that these achievements were an inseparable part of their own heritage — which is why it was crucial for them. Admittedly, exile imposed constrictions and limitations on the life and productivity of the Jewish people so that their inherent potential was not fulfilled in all fields. Positive developments among other peoples, however, were nourished by the influence of Judaism, overtly or unwittingly, and those Jews who were drawn to these developments were — knowingly or unconsciously — fulfilling the mission of their own people; they would restore to it what rightfully belonged to it. This did not mean, of course, that cultural development among other peoples would be similar to Jewish cultural development. Among other peoples, cultural achievements had been severed from the sublime center of a life of authentic belief and had become an end in themselves, as with idolatry. Among the Jewish people these achieve-ments would once again become but a single limb, limited within the organic wholeness of a life of faith, not an independent goal but a means to a nobler perfection. And the restoration of this cultural development to its source in Judaism would thus be a true reforma-tion.

There was a powerful, bold sweep to this theory. Its shortcoming was that it did not correctly interpret the source, thrust and history of European culture, nor did it define the achievements of this culture in their own terms. Therefore it was doubtful whether the theory was capable of objectively dealing with the positive and negative orientations of the culture, for in order to do so, it was not sufficient to "incorporate" it and give it a status within a total theological system that had developed within the continuity of a different spiritual universe. Rather, one had to be familiar with the details of that culture from within. This was the clear advantage of Hirschensohn's view: it was sustained by an objective knowledge of cultural trends in modern Europe, as defined by their own professional disciplines. Of course, by this he was not obligated to agree with all these European trends; on the contrary, on the basis of objective knowledge one could base opposition and criticism or suggest an objective distinction between positive and negative contents; one could also determine on that basis an exact limitation of the cultural development that was desirable for the Jewish people according to criteria found in the Torah. However, his theory not only required empathy toward certain achievements of secular culture, but also an adjustment to its unique methods of thought which afterward must consciously influence a new understanding and a reinterpretation of the Jewish sources.

The general principles which applied to modern culture also applied to that sector of the Jewish people which defined itself as "secular," and to its culture. As noted, Rabbi Kook's theory interpreted the attraction of the "secular" Jew to the fullness of European culture as an essentially positive phenomenon. He was quite daring on this issue. He agreed to secular Zionism's radical concept of the "negation of the diaspora"; even apostasy was interpreted in his theory as a tragic revelation of a faith which could no longer express itself sufficiently through the undeveloped theological concepts of the previous generation. In other words, secularism, negation of the diaspora, and the apostasy of Zionist-national thought were, according to Rabbi Kook's theory, a dialectic manifestation of the desire to raise the true Jewish essence to a more complete level of expression than it had had in Exile. This was a vigorous movement outward, toward the completion of creativity in several areas which could not develop under the conditions of Exile. Although the secular Zionist did not interpret his efforts in this way, it was, according to Rabbi Kook, the true meaning of his endeavors and would become clear to him as well in the process of Zionist realization.

Here was yet another bold sweep of thought which allowed for joint efforts toward the redemption of the Jewish people despite the extreme differences that existed between the religious and the secular regarding the Jewish essence of the Zionist enterprise. Yet the same basic drawback appears again. Rabbi Kook's theory defined the impulse of the secular Zionist and the nature of his efforts from a totally contradictory viewpoint to that of the secular Zionist himself. It purported to know and understand the secular Zionist, and the goal of his actions, in a truer manner than he himself was capable of understanding. It attributed to him a grounding in Judaism of which he himself was not conscious. This was based on a mystical, national concept according to which a Jew could not cut himself off from Judaism, just as a human being could not stop being human. National essence was a fact of birth and could not be changed even if one wanted to forget it — for even the unconscious was a form of knowledge. Ultimate alienation between secular and religious Jews was therefore conceived of as impossible, in the metaphysical sense, and thus the responsibility for joint action was mandated. But it was very doubtful if such a view would permit a relevant confrontation with the positive and negative aspects within the secular community, and it was even doubtful as to whether it allowed for the kind of fraternal fellowship necessary for joint action. In truth, Rabbi Kook's remarks about some modern secular Zionists contained a surprising degree of empathy; that is, those secular Zionists who had a religious Jewish education and retained a deep-rooted heritage of Jewish knowledge and experience, who held on to some faith in the face of their disbelief, and who sought in Zionism a more sublime and complete expression of their Judaism, from the spiritual aspect as well.

Moreover, the process of Zionist realization escalated spiritual confusion within the secular Zionist camp, and the question of spiritual content in Zionist education was pushed to the fore as an increasingly acute issue. Concomitantly, the distance between secular Zionism and Jewish religious heritage was also increasing. This meant that Rabbi Kook was correct to prophesy a crisis in secular Judaism, but the viewpoint with which he interpreted the significance of the Zionist enterprise was foreign and completely incomprehensible to the secular Jew who was engaged in actually making the aspiration real. Indeed, the dialectic of benevolent befriending in which the person being drawn closer could not identify himself with the action, could, in fact, increase the distance. This meant that in order to draw the secular Zionist community near, and in order to confront its orientation, one had to understand that community as it understood itself, and on the basis of such knowledge determine the limits of that which united the two communities and that which distinguished each of them. Such familiarity required an adjustment in patterns of thinking which, in turn, influenced the self-under-standing of religious Zionism. It could not bring people closer "to the fold" without drawing closer to them. Hirschensohn's theory clarified the significance of these two convictions in an exemplary fashion.

What were the hallmarks of this drawing closer to the conceptual system by which secular Judaism defined itself while it remained rooted in general European culture? Hirschensohn rejected the basic assumption on which Rabbi Kook's concept was based, i.e., that Judaism had an inherent ontological reality even before it was defined as a faith and a way of life, and even before it was defined as the national framework of a specific people. According to Rabbi Kook, on the continuum of entities in the world, Judaism held a special qualitative position, a position which was superior to that of other peoples, both in the entire range of cultural creativity and on the spiritual plane. Judaism was the manifestation of the Divine presence in the world, the source of all the substance of cultural originality, and it determined the proper place for that creativity within the total order of human experience. On such a basis it was thus impossible for a Jew to negate his Jewishness, not only because of the fact of his biographical or biological origin, but because of his spiritual quiddity. In fact, this was the basic assumption that allowed Rabbi Kook to be so daring in his positive attitude toward European culture, its scientific, artistic and philosophical achievements, and toward the efforts of secular Zionism in its broad national aspect.

But it was this same assumption which separated him from that culture and endeavor, and militated against his contribution to that culture. To fashion a Torah-based entity within the confines of European culture, one had to recognize that the concepts of that culture also applied to understanding the essence of the Jewish people and the study of its Torah. Thus Hirschensohn objected to these basic assumptions which originated with Rabbi Yehuda Halevi and the Kabbalists. In advancing the approach of the Rambam, Hirschensohn brought Judaism, its people and Torah, into the real historical world. Of course he recognized the national and Torah-based uniqueness of Judaism, and maintained his belief in revelation, but it was a uniqueness envisioned through an understanding of nationality, of religion, and of the role of history in general European culture.

The contrast between Rabbi Hirschensohn and Rabbi Kook is especially evident on the question of animal sacrifice in the future. Hirschensohn's concept of progress embraced humanistic ethics. Rabbi Kook's concept of progress placed them, *ab initio*, on another spiritual plane. There is no doubt that Hirschensohn's humanistic ethics broke down the defensive, fortified wall which afforded Rabbi Kook and his followers a feeling of immunity against the inroads made by the secular culture. But the dismantling of this defensive wall which, at least for Hirschensohn, had only psychological significance was a necessary condition for carrying on a real dialogue with the new culture, whether about what it accepted and affirmed, or about what it rejected and negated. Hirschensohn's great advantage was that he created a Torah-based teaching which could deal objectively with the positive and the negative, with the intellectual horizons of the nationalist Jew who was attached to European culture, philosophy, education, and research, and, above all, with *halakhah*. In all these areas Hirschensohn brought the Torah to the world, and the world to the Torah.

The final general distinction was that Rabbi Kook's theory could support its assumptions — despite the clear contradiction between the definition it offered for Jewish reality in modern times, and the definition accepted by those who were creating this reality — only through the power of belief that the Days of the Messiah were close at hand. The Days of the Messiah meant the divination of a new reality and a new truth which would break through far beyond the horizon of natural historical experience and natural human perception. If, truly, the world were on the verge of a period which would completely change all that was known and understood by man, then the tragic contradiction — between the understanding of the world of Judaism according to Rabbi Kook and the European-secular understanding of the world — could be perceived as merely a dialectic transitional stage in which confrontation took place between the visible old world and a new world which was discernible only to believers.

One could deal with this dialectic transitional stage with a correct interpretation, that is, through education toward a perception of a truth which would be revealed, and through preparation of cultural and national forms for the future which would be completely different from everything that had appeared so real in the present. In other words, the innovative courage of Rabbi Kook's theory by-passed the cultural-social situation in the present, and looked toward the messianic future which, for generations, had been wholly directed toward the eternal vision embodied in the Torah of Judaism. It prepared itself for the change that would come: from a deteriorating Exile toward a supernatural redemption. Thus, even if the theory posited the certainty that the change from Exile to redemption would demand far-reaching changes, these were changes which those living in the present would feel were urgent. From this point of view, Rabbi Kook maintained the expectation that the people would, through the Divine dialectic embodied within it, turn to the Torah; he did not feel the need to bring the Torah into the present. He suffered through the present, and in his suffering he was helping to bring on the future which was close at hand.

As noted, Hirschensohn's theory also reflected an anticipation of imminent redemption. However, this redemption would not break the historical process but would represent a continuous change within its progression. The present was a bridge between the past and the future and thus one must be prepared to meet the future which the present indicated, and not anticipate the future by sliding over the present. On the contrary, one must respond to the expectations and needs that people living in the present felt, according to their own approach. This meant that one could not wait until the people, out of some internal dialectic, turned to the Torah. One must adapt the Torah to the life of the people so that the Torah could once again adapt the people to itself. If steps toward an adjustment to the present were not taken quickly, life in the future would breach the limits of the Torah's authority, and victory would go to the negative values in the new culture.

This difference in assessing the future would seem to explain the divergence between Rabbi Kook and Rabbi Hirschensohn in the direction each took regarding *halakhah*. As audacious as he was ideologically, Rabbi Kook did not show the same daring in the area of *halakhah*. He waited for the messianic change while attempting to prepare the people for its coming, on the educational level. His efforts were chiefly educational-ideological. Rabbi Hirschensohn, however, considered the most important task to be an interpretation of *halakhah*.

Which of the two was historically correct? Obviously such questions do not have an unequivocal answer. The decision depended on the experience which nurtured the messianic faith and determined its coloration. Followers of Rabbi Kook still interpret signs of the time as portents of an imminent super-historical reality, and undertake educational and political activities according to that faith. What can be said is that if one starts from a point of view based on the experience and thought of the majority in the modern-day Jewish community, whether religious or non-religious, and if one tries to deal with the problems of the Jewish character of the State of Israel within this community, then Rabbi Kook's theory appears as a wonderful poem which serves to draw people closer to Torah and love of Israel. It is doubtful, however, if one could find within it guidance on how to continue the cultural, social and political efforts of Zionism, or how to overcome the contradiction between the embodiment of a secular democracy and the vision of a Jewish state according to the Torah. From this point of view, it was Rabbi Hirschensohn's *halakhic* boldness which pointed the way.

Of course, Rabbi Hirschensohn's theory did not remove all the obstacles, nor did it indicate an unobstructed, simple path. In his very boldness to meet the modern era, Hirschensohn took note of a limit at which an unequivocal decision would be required that could cause a split between Torah-observant nationalists and nationalists who rejected the commandments of the Torah. Hirschensohn foresaw a great struggle which he hoped would be a "peaceful" one, one that would end in agreement, and at the time, the hope seemed not without foundation if only his work would find a responsive chord. If only his proposals had been studied and had generated a response, if only followers and supporters had come forward and implemented solutions before stringent standards were set both in lifestyle and in political decisions, perhaps then the tensions between the various camps that were divided over the Jewish character of the state would not have been so sharp. Perhaps a common denominator would have been created, not only in the areas of settlement and politics, but also in cultural and social areas. Perhaps the argument between "religious" and "secular" would have been less unvarying and barren, more relevant and fruitful.

In any event, matters developed differently. The multi-faceted, ideological ferment of many creative individuals in both the religious and secular camps was not expressed in public life. On the contrary, each camp backed the other into a set and stubborn position; they acquiesced to a partnership in the political-pragmatic arena through a compact in which they agreed they would not agree in everything concerning the Jewish character of the Zionist enterprise in Eretz Israel. Perhaps that was the basic reason that Hirschensohn's efforts did not gain proper attention. Was it purposefully ignored because it presented a difficult challenge for the immediate present in the practical areas of politics, society and education? It was obvious that the creation of a network of relationships between the religious and secular camps in Zionism, on the basis of an agreement not to adopt a consensus about the Jewish essence of the Zionist enterprise, was much simpler for the time being, and it was natural that the political leadership, in weighing short-term considerations, would prefer the solution which appeared easiest for the moment.

Unintentionally — and ironically so — Rabbi Kook provided a deep psychological justification and even a sublime theological justification for an uncomplicated solution. If the dialectic of Divine Providence which was revealed in the history of the Jewish people would restore secular Zionism to its true, national-religious source, there was no need to create a *halakhic* infrastructure with which to reach an agreement with the secular community on current questions to which they took diametrically opposite stands. The national-religious camp had only to defend its positions, expand the horizons of its understanding, increase its spiritual influence, and anticipate the messianic moment of repentance. Rabbi Hirschensohn's view completely contravened the human tendency to postpone a decision. On the contrary, he pointed out the critical responsibility to confront questions concerning the Jewish essence of the Zionist project and the necessity of dealing with these questions immediately, lest the hour be lost, and the split become an irreversible fact.

The reality which developed after the establishment of the state make the questions which Hirschensohn raised even more complex and grave than he could have foreseen during his lifetime. Should one want to study his theory and act on it now, the solutions that Rabbi Hirschensohn advanced would be found insufficient for the contemporary scene. On the other hand, it would appear that the relationships between the secular camp and the religious camp in Zionism have reached a turning point. The framework of practical arrangements which had been forged by ignoring the question of the Jewish identity of the state cannot stand for much longer under the pressure of basic and practical problems which have remained unresolved. If there is not an immediate stirring to search for solutions, it is doubtful if it will be possible to prevent the bitter results of a split between the secular and religious.

It is for this reason that the author attaches very great importance to Rabbi Hirschensohn's work. In principle, his approach contains an inherent prospect which is perhaps the only chance to foster a Torah way of life that approximates conditions of contemporary reality and the assumptions of modern culture. At the same time it lays a foundation for a national consensus that will enable both sectors to struggle responsibly and objectively with each other, perhaps even to evolve pragmatic solutions that are not faulty temporary compromises, but a firmly paved road.

Note

1. The discussion below on the theories of Rabbi Kook is of a general nature; therefore, specific references have not been given. For more detail in interpreting the views of Rabbi Kook according to the author, see my book, *The Individual Jew and Judaism* (Hebrew), Part II, Ch. 3, "Secularism from a Religious Viewpoint" (Tel Aviv: Am Oved, 1974).

INDEX

155

ABOUT THE AUTHOR

Professor Eliezer Schweid was born in Jerusalem in 1929. He served in the Palmach during Israel's War of Independence and joined Kibbutz Zorea after the war. Attending Hebrew University, he specialized in Jewish history and philosophy, receiving his Ph.D. in 1962. He has been teaching at Hebrew University and other Israeli universities since 1963, and became a full Professor in 1982. Professor Schweid is a Fellow and Vice President of the Jerusalem Center for Public Affairs. He is married and has three children.

Professor Schweid has been involved in a number of Jewish education projects in Israel and has published many papers on medieval and modern Jewish philosophy, Hebrew literature, and Zionism, as well as contributing to Israeli journals on current affairs. He is the author of a number of books on Jewish philosophy and literature. His most recent book in English is *Jewish Thought in the Twentieth Century — An Introduction* (Atlanta: U.S.F. Studies in the History of Judaism. The Scholars Press, 1992).